The Non-Monogamy Journal

by the same author

The Anxious Person's Guide to Non-Monogamy
Your Guide to Open Relationships, Polyamory and Letting Go
Foreword by Kathy G. Slaughter, LCSW
ISBN 978 1 83997 213 3
eISBN 978 1 83997 214 0

of related interest

Monogamy? In this Economy?
Finances, Childrearing, and Other Practical Concerns of Polyamory
Laura Boyle
ISBN 978 1 80501 118 7
eISBN 978 1 80501 119 4

Queer Sex
A Trans and Non-Binary Guide to Intimacy, Pleasure and Relationships
Juno Roche
ISBN 978 1 78592 406 4
eISBN 978 1 78450 770 1

How to Understand Your Sexuality
A Practical Guide for Exploring Who You Are
Meg-John Barker and Alex Iantaffi
Illustrated by Jules Scheele
ISBN 978 1 78775 618 2
eISBN 978 1 78775 619 9

The Non-Monogamy Journal

90+ Scenarios and Questions to Define Boundaries and Make Polyamory Work for You

LOLA PHOENIX

Foreword by Kathy G. Slaughter, LCSW

Jessica Kingsley Publishers
London and Philadelphia

First published in Great Britain in 2025 by Jessica Kingsley Publishers
An imprint of John Murray Press

1

A CIP catalogue record for this title is available from the British Library and the Library of Congress

ISBN 978 1 80501 422 5
eISBN 978 1 80501 423 2

Printed and bound in Great Britain by Bell & Bain Limited

Jessica Kingsley Publishers' policy is to use papers that are natural, renewable and recyclable products and made from wood grown in sustainable forests. The logging and manufacturing processes are expected to conform to the environmental regulations of the country of origin.

Jessica Kingsley Publishers
Carmelite House
50 Victoria Embankment
London EC4Y 0DZ

www.jkp.com

John Murray Press
Part of Hodder & Stoughton Limited
An Hachette UK Company

The authorised representative in the EEA is Hachette Ireland, 8 Castlecourt Centre, Dublin 15, D15 XTP3, Ireland (email: info@hbgi.ie)

For anyone who has felt like they needed a helicopter to take them to safety.

Contents

Foreword

Ethical non-monogamy promises a life of abundant love and autonomy. Alongside these benefits, it also brings up so much uncertainty. That uncertainty comes from pursuing a different type of relationship than you grew up expecting to experience.

According to the Western culture we live and love within, there is only one type of valid romantic relationship: an exclusive commitment to only one other person, hopefully someone of the opposite sex. There are countless millions of words on the internet and in self-help books and magazine articles, as well as fictional movies and TV shows, that give inspiration and instruction about that type of relationship. Between public figures and fictional characters, you absorb hundreds of examples by the time you reach adulthood.

Now you've decided to give non-monogamy a whirl. That means shifting to an entirely new paradigm of relating. One that you know much less about. That lack of knowledge and outside support leads to uncertainty for many, even if they're truly excited about embracing this new way of thinking and loving.

Coping with uncertainty can look like seeking reassurance from others or understanding more about the situation. If you're new to non-monogamy, both of those might be in short supply. It's hard to reassure yourself that everything is going to be alright in your relationship, when the very foundation of it has been altered. Or perhaps you've joined someone who already practises non-monogamy, and you're wondering how to feel secure in a relationship that will never become exclusive. Or maybe you've decided on your own to forgo monogamy, and yet worry about how that will impact those you want to date. Perhaps you've heard you ought to know what kind of open relationship you want, and you have no idea!

Understanding more about the situation can also prove elusive because non-monogamy is still a relatively new phenomenon, at least in terms of visibility in more mainstream spaces and in its modern incarnation. There's not that many publicly visible possibility models to observe and learn from. And most mainstream relationship advice will actually hamper your ability to enjoy non-monogamy!

So, you're lost. How can you even begin to understand what's to come?

That's where this workbook comes in.

Based on Lola's years of experience giving advice to real people dealing with real situations, this workbook makes it super simple to take all that uncertainty and turn it into answers. Your answers, based on your values and your desires.

When you're first starting out in non-monogamy, it can be pretty all-consuming. If you like to learn and prepare ahead of time, then it can be incredibly hard to imagine all the different ways shifting to non-monogamy can impact your life and your relationships. Many veterans and influencers will tell you to imagine what you want your relationships to look like. Great advice, but it's extremely hard to implement. This workbook provides a much easier way to approach all of this.

For me, it took a few years of practising polyamory, attending all the conferences, and reading all the books to put it together – to begin to understand the range of possibilities before me, and to begin to understand what I wanted in a holistic and nuanced way. Lola's work will let you skip that part. Within this workbook, you'll find prompts, questions and real-life examples to support your reflections. By working cover to cover, you'll be prepared for just about anything that comes your way.

By the end of this workbook, you'll understand more about what matters to you within your intimate relationships. You'll know what boundaries enhance your sense of wellbeing, and how to deal with new relationship types, like metamours. You'll consider how you want to disclose (or not) that you practise non-monogamy. And there will be so many invitations to explore how your feelings might surface.

Because in my experience, non-monogamy will bring any hidden insecurities roaring to the forefront. There's something about setting aside the veneer of safety that a promise to be exclusive can bring that just rattles people. Especially if you're kind of forging a different path on your own.

As you begin to spend time with others, and your partners have other significant others, you'll likely discover that you have many beliefs about relationships that you didn't even know existed. They were formed within you by the monocentric culture we live in. It can be incredibly difficult to sort out which beliefs will still fit in this new open relationship paradigm, and which ones have to go.

I hear some version of that concern constantly as a therapist who works with all sorts of people in non-monogamous set-ups. Professionally, I've worked with a variety of people pursuing different kinds of non-monogamy. They all struggled with knowing what was 'reasonable or acceptable' in this new context.

In my endless quest for deeper understanding of how to make empowered decisions about non-monogamy, I came across Lola's column years ago. I devoured their content. Here was someone else living with and writing about handling non-monogamy from a pragmatic and grounded point of view. Everything they wrote sliced through the uncertainty in my own mind, clarified a question I'd been chewing on, or affirmed a conclusion I had already made.

Over the years, Lola's column and podcast brought many questions forward for consideration. In time, certain concepts began to really crystallize into a particular approach to non-monogamy for me, based in pragmatic responses to real scenarios and my own values. This workbook brings many of these scenarios to you, providing you with a great opportunity to bring clarity to your non-monogamous experience and leave uncertainty behind.

Kathy G. Slaughter, LCSW, trauma and sexuality therapist

Introduction

I've been writing Non-Monogamy Help as an advice column and a podcast for around seven years now and I've considered myself some form of non-monogamous since 2010. From both giving advice and my own experience, I know that there are some situations that you really don't know how you'll respond to until you're in them. With monogamy, we have what I call a 'cultural script'. We see monogamy demonstrated in our lives, in the media and all around us. So many of the situations that we come across in our lives, we're able to have some form of a model for. With non-monogamy, this is often not the case.

Sexual, romantic and emotional monogamy is actually quite a new thing (in many societies, married men have been free to have extramarital affairs with little consequence depending on their station), non-monogamy is a more recent practice, with little in the way of examples for people to follow. Many of the situations that arise are new ones that people aren't used to tackling, so if someone needs to deal with a problem in a relationship, this can often be an additional issue.

My goal with my first book, *The Anxious Person's Guide to Non-Monogamy*, was to provide something for people just starting out in non-monogamy and also people who found their anxiety particularly stoked by non-monogamy and needed to hear from someone who felt similarly. In that book, at the end of each chapter, I provided a couple of exercises people could do on their own or with partners to help them work through anxiety as well as set themselves up as best as they could if they were starting out.

Here, my goal is to provide you with a wide range of scenarios you can think on by yourself or with partners and consider how you might respond.

My hope is that the exploration of these scenarios will help you better understand yourself, your approach to non-monogamy, and where your boundaries are. Quite often I say – and have experienced – that sometimes we don't know we want a boundary until one has already been crossed.

These scenarios and questions are designed to help you consider your positions on different aspects. If you are running through these with a partner, remember that you do not have to agree completely on every position. It is possible to disagree on something and decide to put it down instead of arguing back and forth about it ad nauseam.

Some of the scenarios won't apply or can't apply to your life, some of them will, and some of them you may have to tweak a little to get them to apply to you in a way that's useful, but hopefully all of them contain something that will help you explore your ideals and boundaries, and maybe even find your anchor – which is a term I have coined to describe a personal reason you are interested in pursuing non-monogamy.

As I always say, I hope this helps and good luck.

HOW TO USE THIS BOOK

Each page will contain either a particular issue that often comes up within polyamory or describe a particular scenario. You can use this book on your own or with a partner. You can write down what you would do in these circumstances, you can talk it out, or you can just think about it to yourself.

Consider how the situation may or may not apply to you – not all the situations or problems will – and what your key triggers might be about that situation. I've grouped these situations and considerations into themes, which may help you explore subjects that you might also struggle with. You can go straight to a specific theme, go through the scenarios in order, or even roll a dice and see which scenario you get. Since they not designed to necessarily be explored in order, some concepts may be repeated for clarity.

The themes are:

- Boundaries: This theme can help you explore boundaries you might have in non-monogamy regarding disclosure, metamours (your partner's other partners), who you date, who you are 'out' to, and how you might handle objections to who or how you date.

- Structure: Figuring out the ways to structure relationships, how to label yourself, and what you might do as relationships progress can often be an afterthought for some people, but this theme can help you explore some of those ideas. While not all these scenarios may be applicable to you, they might help you explore how you feel about different things.
- Emotions: It is understandable that polyamory causes some big emotions to surface, and trying to figure out how to deal with your partner's emotions and those boundaries can be difficult. This theme can help you focus on situations where you might have to think about how you process your or your partner's emotions.
- Compromises: Every relationship involves compromise and not every single relationship is going to be always equally balanced. This theme can help you think about ways that inequity or differences might crop up and how you might balance your own needs with your partners' needs even when those might directly conflict.
- Sexuality and Infidelity: Sexuality is a huge part of many people's relationships for understandable reasons, and this theme will help you navigate some basic rules for how you might negotiate sexual boundaries as well as other situations that could crop up that may challenge your current understandings, and help you consider ways in which you may compromise.

Theme: Boundaries

SCENARIO 1: DISCLOSURE

One of the trickiest aspects in polyamory for new people is deciding when to disclose and what to disclose with a partner. Not everyone is able to pinpoint the moment when they start to feel 'more' for someone than 'just a friend' and some people may not feel that their feelings are so easily compartmentalized.

Disclosure is also when you put your money where your mouth is, so to speak, and you actually end up doing what you're talking about. Telling your partner that you have an interest in someone or have done something with someone is the moment of truth – for them as well as you. Are they going to have a bad reaction? What happens if they do? Many times, people make rules around disclosure either to prevent themselves from being accused of cheating or to help recognize when their partner is slipping away – though these rules very rarely actually stop someone from losing their partner.

Things to Consider

Work through the following questions on the theme of 'disclosure'.

- When do you think is the best time to disclose something to your partner?
- What do you think you should disclose?
- Does it have to be official, or can the rules be looser?
- If you find yourself wanting rigidity here, is it because you're trying to prevent something?
- Where is the line for you between waiting to disclose and 'cheating'?
- What happens when you don't disclose something you were meant to?

....

....

....

....

....

SCENARIO 2: NEW RELATIONSHIP ENERGY

Even if you've never been non-monogamous, you will likely have encountered what's called 'new relationship energy'. It's a phenomenon where someone gets excited about a new relationship and becomes a little obsessed with it, sometimes neglecting their other relationships. This happens even in monogamy where someone becomes part of 'a couple' and tends to ignore their friends, especially since most of us live in a culture that tells us our romantic relationships should take precedence over all other things.

Situation

Imagine you have a partner who has practically dropped off the face of the earth in terms of their communication. It's not someone you live with or necessarily speak to every day, but it is someone you used to have regular communication with and now you are seeing a sharp, steep decline in that communication. Imagine this partner has also missed a recent important milestone in your relationship that was very important to you, leaving you feeling especially hurt.

How do you address this lack with your partner? Can you identify the point in a situation like this where being ignored would become too much for you to handle?

....

....

....

....

....

....

....

....

....

....

SCENARIO 3: CONFIDING IN METAMOURS

It's normal – and in fact a good idea – to confide in friends about your relationships. One of the 'red flags' (though that term is often misused) I would consider in any relationship is a partner who is attempting to alienate you from your friendship group. Confiding in our friends helps us recognize when situations around us aren't working for us in ways we sometimes can't even see. However, for a lot of polyamorous people, if you don't have polyamorous friends, it can be a struggle to feel like they can provide you with good advice – especially if they think just being polyamorous is a one-way ticket to heartbreak town.

Metamours, or your partner's other partners that you don't date, can become good friends because quite often people tend to date people who have things in common. But a metamour friend is different to a friend who has no stake in your relationship and doesn't intimately know your partner. Confiding in metamours about things can be difficult for them and it can sometimes make them feel in the middle.

Situation

You are very good friends with your metamour and would stay friends even if you ended up splitting up with your partner. You both have a lot in common and talk pretty frequently. Now, you're going through a lot in your life in general and struggling to find support. None of your other friends are polyamorous and a few of them, though they don't say it out loud, think that polyamory 'doesn't work'.

Some of the problems, though not all, are with your shared partner. You struggle to identify and articulate the problems you're having, and you desperately want to ask your metamour if they also struggle with similar things in the relationship they have with your shared partner.

Do you confide in your metamour in this case? What type of information would you feel comfortable talking about? If you were the metamour hearing this, would you want your metamour to talk to you and about what? How might this discussion help or hurt your relationship and the relationships you have with your shared partner?

SCENARIO 4: MENTAL HEALTH DISCLOSURE

As someone who struggled with anxiety for years, I know that mental health conditions can have a huge impact on our day-to-day lives and the way we do relationships. Diagnoses may help us gain access to the medical care we need to address our situations, but may not necessarily be the ideal path for all. Many people are unable to afford therapy interventions, and we live in a society that doesn't exactly encourage us to prioritize our mental health.

Within polyamory communities, there can be added stigma when you have a mental health condition, diagnosis or not. Comments like 'don't stick your dick in crazy' and the concept that polyamory is 'harder' or a level above monogamy can make many people with mental health struggles feel like, to put it bluntly, they aren't sane enough to be a good partner.

Situation

You have a mental health condition with a formal diagnosis that you had to get to access the medical care you needed to address your condition. You are currently doing the advised amount of therapy and/or taking the medications that you feel you need to manage the symptoms of your condition.

Your mental health condition has in the past impacted your life and your relationships, but overall, you feel like this is something you're able to manage provided the right support, compassion and understanding of the people around you. You learn that your partner has disclosed your mental health diagnosis to a metamour during a time when you had been under duress to 'explain' your behaviour to them.

Before this, you had no set rule against your partner telling someone else about your diagnosis but you now feel embarrassed and angry that they didn't think to get your consent first. You aren't trying to hide your condition from anyone, but something about this doesn't sit right with you.

Explore how you might address something like this and, if you have a mental health condition or a partner with a mental health condition, what your boundaries are around the disclosure of that medical condition to metamours, family, friends and other people involved in your life. Does it change if there is an official diagnosis?

SCENARIO 5: MEETING FAMILY

Families are difficult to navigate in any type of relationship and there are many perspectives on the best way to manage families. Having come from a difficult family background, I assumed for a long time that someone having family in their life was always a good thing, but it can be incredibly complicated, and the added stress of introducing the concept of polyamory, which might not be culturally accepted, to your family can add further complications.

People can also have several different feelings about how involved they would like to be in meeting and engaging with their partner's family members. For some, this may not even be an issue – they have no interest in it, or they don't have any living family or any connection to family that would come up. But for others, fitting into and meeting their partner's family may be something that they see as very important. Because monogamy-centric society often assumes that fitting into each other's family will always happen and will always work well, sometimes this topic goes undiscussed until it becomes an issue.

Situation

For whatever reason, it is important for you to meet and fit in with a family of at least one of your partners. The partner you have who plays the biggest role in your life, in terms of who you spend the most time with and whether you're considering living together or sharing assets together, does not have a good connection with their family.

In this situation, assume either they have no contact with their family and have no interest in reconnecting unless there are drastic changes, or they have some connection with family but you don't particularly feel that connection is healthy or good for them or for you.

How would you navigate this situation in particular? Explore also how your family may react if you bring more than one partner home or introduce the concept of polyamory, if you haven't yet. How do you deal with meeting families – ones that are welcoming and ones that may not be? What is your expectation or hope for your partner's involvement when you're dealing with their family?

SCENARIO 6: DATING FRIENDS

Many polyamory communities are small worlds, especially in cities that aren't so big, where we may struggle to find polyamorous people to date with. The irony of the situation is that wanting to date more than one person romantically and ethically doesn't widen your dating pool. It makes it a lot smaller than you'd think.

However, there are a lot of people who don't know that they are polyamorous because they've never explored it, and people who, when they consider the idea, are intrigued by it. Polyamory can be one of those things that people don't really consider as an option earlier in their life, so they often don't have a chance to have any strong opinions about it. There are some people who are open to trying polyamory but are not within the polyamory community. Many polyamorous people prefer to date other people who are not just considering polyamory but who have some experience. What this means is that, because the dating and social circle is so small, many polyamorous people end up dating their partner's friends.

Within monogamy, many people have feelings about their friends dating their exes or their exes dating their friends, and when someone decides to try polyamory, some of these feelings can cross over or it can be confusing to know how to respond in these situations.

Situation

You have a friend who feels like family to you, and you talk almost every day. Over the past couple of weeks, you've noticed that they seem a little bit distant from you. At first, you brush this off as something you might be imagining but as time goes on it gets harder and harder to ignore.

Finally, when talking in a cafe, your friend confesses something. They are attracted to one of your partners, and they confessed this to your partner a few days ago. Your partner knows they are a close friend of yours, but hasn't yet told you about the confession or mentioned anything about this friend previously.

How do you feel about this disclosure? How do you feel about your partner dating your friends in general? Would you prefer it if your partner had told you this or your friend? Explore what sorts of boundaries you may or may not have around dating friends.

SCENARIO 7: UNSPOKEN BOUNDARIES

I can't recall exactly when I first heard the term 'situationship', but it speaks to a wider phenomenon that I think is becoming more popular. A 'situationship' is defined as a not-quite relationship where the people involved are not officially together but are usually involved more sexually than romantically in a casual way.

While I'm sure there are people who function better than others when boundaries between friendship and relationship are hazier, I do think there is a difference between deliberately choosing a relationship with those boundaries (or lack thereof) and falling into a situation where you have no boundaries because you're too afraid to lose what you do have to say anything.

Whenever we're starting in polyamory, we often struggle to assert our own needs – or at least I did – especially when we're not quite sure what those needs are just yet. The grotesque spectre of jealousy and having to prove you can 'handle' polyamory further confounds this. It's very easy to dismiss a feeling as jealousy just because you're not quite sure what it is otherwise. I believe that for some people, when boundaries are fuzzier, knowing when to speak up can be more confusing.

Situation

You've been speaking to someone you very much like for about six months. You're not too keen on long-distance relationships since you've been burned in the past, so you haven't officially declared yourselves in a relationship, but it's clear, you feel, that if you were in the same town, you would be dating.

For more than a year, you've been planning on moving cities. You had put that on your dating profile and looked for people in the city you are moving to, which is where this person lives. You're just two months shy of moving to this city when they ask you to check their social media profile. On it you can see they are now listed as dating another person and it's not specified as an open relationship (and that is an option on this social network).

At first, you're surprised. They've never mentioned this person before. Not going on a date with them, not being interested in them – nothing. It seems sudden but you chalk it up to jealousy and offer an olive branch and say that you'd be glad to meet this partner and offer to send a friend request.

The person you like asks you not to do that, says they prefer if you meet in person and seeing as you only have two months to wait, this doesn't seem like such a huge deal at the time. Your alarms are going off, but you assume you are just being jealous.

What do you do in this situation? How might you manage little flags like this where something seems off but it's easy to dismiss it as jealousy? How do you feel about this request from a partner in this situation?

SCENARIO 8: BROKEN PROMISES

While there are a lot of people in polyamory communities and polyamory media who rail against 'rules' and make it seem like you have to be absolutely okay with almost anything in order to be 'good' at polyamory, I think there are sometimes things we can ask for or requests we can make, which don't have to be considered 'rules', but can help bridge the gap and make things a little easier for our partners and ourselves.

One example of this was that I had, not a 'rule', but an agreement with an ex that when they were spending nights away from me, I could have a five-minute goodnight call. In the earlier days of our relationship (we were together for about six years), this was extremely helpful for me. As our relationship matured, I needed this less.

It's okay to want to have a little bit of a safety net during new situations but it's also important not to coddle yourself into a false sense of safety. Requests can't be designed to prevent things they can't prevent. Initially with the same ex, I requested that they not sleep with anyone they just met because I believed this was unsafe because of the risk of sexually transmitted diseases (STIs).

This wouldn't prevent them from catching STIs, however, since STIs don't care how long you know somebody. Instead, we renegotiated that they would at least ask people if they had been tested recently and agreed upon our definition of how recent the test needed to be. Later, we renegotiated the protections we used with each other so that their interactions with other people with regard to casual sex weren't so limited. Though I sometimes felt uncomfortable about the risk of STIs (something which can't be totally avoided), this worked for us because we could come to an agreement.

Situation

You have asked your partner for something that's designed to help comfort you in the difficulties you occasionally have with polyamory. It doesn't constitute 'cheating' or anything serious if this request is not honoured, but you know it would hurt if it wasn't honoured.

Your partner, while under the influence of substances, did not honour your request and is considerably remorseful about their failure to do so.

However, they feel that the request is not something that is workable for them going forward and they want to renegotiate.

How do you manage a situation like this, either as the partner making the request or the partner receiving it? Does it depend on what the request is regarding? Think about requests you can see yourself making or have made in the past.

SCENARIO 9: DISCLOSING POLYAMORY

Because monogamy is a cultural normal and polyamory isn't something many people have considered, it is possible that someone could be very well suited to polyamory or even want polyamory without ever really knowing it until they're introduced to the concept. And just like most other lifestyle situations, unless someone has a strong feeling in the pro or con area, it's hard to know if this is going to be the right decision for you until you try it. That means that when people decide to join dating sites or naturally meet someone and flirt with them, it can be difficult to know when and how to disclose that you already have a partner or partners or that you're interested in polyamory in general. People have an understandable fear of 'scaring off' people or being assumed to be a cheater.

Some people swear off dating anyone without any 'experience' in polyamory and while I understand the rationale behind it, I think that this isn't always the best or even the most reasonable choice for everyone. My rule has always been that, where it makes sense, I'd rather be honest as soon as possible to avoid wasting anyone's time. If someone is going to be scared by the mention of polyamory, I think the chances of them wanting to be open to it are too small.

Things to Consider

Work through the following questions on the theme of 'disclosing polyamory':

- Do you prefer to put on your dating profiles that you're 'polyamorous', 'non-monogamous', etc.? Why?
- Do you prefer to wait to disclose? Why?
- How do you handle meeting someone in 'the wild' who shows an interest in you? When do you disclose? If it is a casual encounter or a one-night stand do you feel you need to disclose?
- Are you open to dating people who are completely new to polyamory and introduced to the concept by you? If so, why? If not, why?

....

....

SCENARIO 10: METAMOUR DETAILS

As discussed previously, our friends are important parts of our lives, and sometimes provide invaluable feedback on aspects of our relationships that we might not otherwise be aware of because we're too close to the situation.

It's natural, then, for us to want to talk to our partners about our other relationships and it's also natural for them to want to know when we're stressed or struggling, what we're stressed about and why. But it can be difficult when it comes to polyamory because, whereas a friend can be a somewhat neutral third party, when your partner confides in you about a struggle they have with a metamour, if there is a conflict of interest or a clash between your needs and your metamour's needs, what your partner tells you can affect how you feel about their other relationship.

In addition, monogamous-centric culture blended in with a bit of consumer capitalism often leads us to believe that our partners choose us because we're 'the best', so when you witness your partner choosing other people who you might not consider to be 'the best', it can bring up a lot of feelings about the decisions your partner makes and why they make them – and what that can mean about you.

Situation

Your partner is really struggling with a metamour and confides in you about it frequently. You haven't yet met this metamour, but they've been dating for a few months and the relationship between them doesn't seem healthy to you. Your partner is often stressed and even though you haven't asked to hear any details, you can't help but ask them how they are doing and give them the space to vent.

As a result, you know a lot of information about this metamour and their personal history – more than they know about you. Your partner doesn't express any desire to end the relationship and you still find pockets of time together to enjoy your relationship without talking about your metamour, but it is still something that comes up again and again.

How would you feel about this situation? Would you want to meet the metamour? Would you want any boundaries in place in terms of what your partner could disclose about the other people they date? How might the discussions you have had impact your relationship? Also put yourself in the position of the partner with the stressful metamour – what would you do if your partner put boundaries down around discussing your situation with them?

SCENARIO 11: DATING FAMILY

Outside of television shows, I'm not sure how often your partner dating your family members could happen. But I have lived in a very small town and close-knit communities where everyone knows everyone's business so I could see the issue of partners dating family members becoming a problem for some – and especially as polyamorous communities and polyamorous dating pools can be so small, and we don't often know everything about our family members' personal lives, it's something that's worth thinking about.

A lot of monogamous people would, understandably within this culture, have boundaries around their family dating their exes or their exes dating their family, but I think if pressed to really explain why, some people might actually struggle to articulate the problem. Generally, I think it comes from the fact that for many people, family relationships are very much set in stone and feel inescapable. It's not easy to disconnect from family, so the idea of something coming along that might threaten that is an understandable worry for many people.

Situation

You have a large extended family that you have a positive relationship with and see regularly. You have several partners; some you live with and some you don't live with. A partner that you do not live with randomly matched with a cousin of yours on a dating site and they hit it off; your cousin is now interested in trying polyamory.

What would be your feelings around this situation? Would it change if it were a partner you were living with? Would it change if it were a closer relative than a cousin? Explore your feelings around your partners dating family members.

. . . .

. . . .

. . . .

. . . .

. . . .

SCENARIO 12: SAYING 'I LOVE YOU'

Everyone has different boundaries around how they feel about saying 'I love you' in relationships. While I do sometimes feel that people are a little too quick to label things 'red flags', I do think general cultural boundaries around saying 'I love you' too soon within relationships make a lot of sense.

While we know that 'love' is something that typically doesn't happen at first sight, what 'love' is to each person and how we express it can be wildly different. This creates unique potential obstacles within polyamory where we have a vested interest in understanding the relationships that our partners have with other people. Thus our personal differences in what we consider 'love' to mean and how we represent it can create a lot of anxiety when we are trying to understand the nature of our partners' relationships.

Add that to the fact that not every polyamorous relationship has the same type of milestones we've come to learn as typical within relationships from the culture around us and it makes things complicated.

Things to Consider

Work through the following questions on the theme of saying 'I love you' within relationships:

- When have you said 'I love you' in relationships?
- Do you have feelings about when it is 'too soon' to say 'I love you' and why?
- What do you feel is different, if anything, in polyamory?
- How do you feel in general about the concept of 'like' versus 'love'?

....

....

....

....

....

....

SCENARIO 13: SECOND-HAND CENSORSHIP

When there are situations that involve people who are called 'abusive', it does seem like the concept of veto power or controlling how or when a partner interacts with someone else goes out the window a little. Understandably, people may struggle with what they should do if someone within their polyamorous circle is labelled as 'abusive', and they want to respect any hurt parties involved but also want to keep their friendship.

The pressure to no longer associate with people who are deemed to have caused harm is huge in many communities, and it becomes even more difficult if you have feelings for that person or feel like your dating options are not very widespread. If you're removed from the situation in that you don't even know the hurt parties involved, it can make things even more complicated.

Situation

You have been speaking to someone for a few months and it's one of the newest and best relationships you've had in a long time. You haven't managed to set aside time to meet up just yet, but you've had some very good, extensive conversations and you feel very close to this person.

You have another partner that you're living with and have been with for a few years. They bring a concern to you from a metamour about the person you've been speaking to. Your metamour says this person is toxic and abusive and has essentially threatened to break up with your partner if you choose to date this person. Your partner is concerned for your wellbeing but also feels frustrated by this situation and isn't sure what to do.

What would you do in this situation? Would it change if you had an ex who you felt was very abusive and your metamour began dating them? Do you feel their request is unreasonable? Why?

....

....

....

....

SCENARIO 14: INTRODUCING POLYAMORY

The option of dating only within non-monogamous communities is only available to specific groups and even in those situations, many people may find themselves having a crush or a desire for someone in a space that is not specifically non-monogamous or polyamorous.

While attitudes towards polyamory vary wildly depending on where you live and, as far as I know, there is not very much social data on people's perceptions of non-monogamy, I think that most people's opinion of 'open relationships' – which tends to be the easiest way many people can conceptualize polyamory – is that they fundamentally 'don't work'. I don't think the average person really sees non-monogamy as a realistic option for them to pursue.

Some people may be 'impressed' by someone's ability to 'do non-monogamy' but that sort of morbid curiosity doesn't always feel very much like admiration or encouragement. For this reason, outside of it being openly discouraged (especially for women) in more conservative environments, the challenge of being the one to introduce polyamory to a potential crush may not be something a lot of people want to be responsible for.

Situation

You have an interest in someone through a shared community that is not non-monogamy focused and you're pretty sure they have an interest in you. You have one other partner, but it's not known within this community that you're not 'single'. Assume also that if you lost access to this community for whatever reason, it wouldn't be hugely detrimental to you. Also assume that while you do have an interest in this person, you can't say for sure if you would be good partners.

How would you go about introducing the subject to a person you have an interest in? Do you think there is anything unethical about avoiding telling this person about your partner until a certain point? When does it become unethical to avoid telling them? How would your approach change if the community you had access to played a bigger role in your life or if there was a personal risk involved in others knowing you are non-monogamous?

SCENARIO 15: CONTROL

Many people within polyamorous communities are understandably hesitant about the idea of their relationships with others being 'controlled' by their partners, intentionally or otherwise. Especially if there are interpersonal struggles with establishing boundaries and sticking to those boundaries, it can be difficult if, for example, your partner has a very large emotional reaction to another partner to not feel there is an element of being 'controlled' by their emotions.

Even when we have decided that things like 'vetoes' are not allowed, if our desire is for our partners to get along but our partners do not actually like each other, this can create a strain that some people struggle to ignore. I often encourage people to understand not only that the reactions and emotions of other partners aren't always mandates or attempts to 'control' anyone, but also that we often don't realize that there are plenty of other parts of life that can unavoidably exert the same type of 'control' over our relationships. For example, the relationships we have with our family and friends – if they dislike our partners or don't get along – can also feel like they 'control' our relationships. Our jobs and the demands of having to ensure our own survival in society have 'control' over our free time and even our ability to afford dating or moving out of a place we share with partners. There are many, many things out of our immediate control that can have a profound impact on our relationships.

Things to Consider

Work through the following questions on the theme of 'control':

- What experiences have you had of other people in your life having 'control' over your relationships?
- Do you struggle with feeling 'controlled' by the strong emotions of others?
- Can you identify the non-relationship aspects of your life that may 'control' or impact your relationships now and in the future?

SCENARIO 16: EMOTIONAL CONFUSION

Many people struggle to identify and process their own emotions, which can sometimes make it difficult if people in polyamory have agreed to notify their partners or keep them in the loop whenever their relationships progress in any way. Even if you don't have a rule where you need your partner's permission to escalate a relationship, it makes sense for your partners to want to know when things might change in their relationship with you.

I typically encourage people to focus a little less on trying to identify the moments when they feel their emotions change for someone and instead focus on the physical aspects of relationships and how they might change. However, if you have a partner who doesn't have a strong understanding of their emotions and, from your point of view, it seems like the relationship they are in is 'progressing' and they aren't saying anything to you, it can be difficult and confusing. It's important to remember that not everyone processes emotions the same way, and if someone isn't fantastic about recognizing their own emotions, they may not have been trying to hide anything or being dishonest.

Situation

You're dating someone who is a bit more emotionally distant than you're used to. While you prefer to discuss your feelings, your partner does a lot more internal processing than you. In the process of dating others, you tend to notice when the relationships your partner has with others are getting deeper before your partner really has a chance to talk to you about it.

Although there is no rule in your relationship to notify each other before anything progresses, there is something about the situation that makes you feel anxious. Your partner does eventually end up talking to you about their feelings for others, but this is well past the point when you noticed they were getting closer to the other person.

How do you handle a situation like this? Does this bother you? What about your partner being less connected with their emotions might cause you difficulty? Or are you the partner who is more disconnected to your emotions?

SCENARIO 17: DATING EXES

Within monogamy, the idea of someone you know dating your ex tends to cause a lot of people understandable pause, especially when it comes to our friends dating our exes. There are a lot of reasons why people might feel awkward about their friends and other people they know dating their exes, which can range from being anxious about comparisons to some of society's older ideas about ownership in relationships.

However, within polyamory, especially considering how small communities can be and how frequently people tend to find themselves attracted to similar people, the problem of whether or not to date exes becomes a somewhat larger issue. Even though who you're attracted to isn't up to you, if you're already struggling to find polyamorous people and manage to find yourself attracted to someone who your partner used to date or see, it may be quite difficult to feel that you can pass up the opportunity, compared to similar situations that may pop up when you're monogamous.

Situation

You're dating someone who recently broke up with a partner that they live with. You got to know your metamour through your partner and developed a fun friendship that you've nurtured for a while. Over the past few months, before the breakup, you've been noticing yourself developing feelings for your metamour.

The breakup between your metamour and your partner wasn't acrimonious, but it has impacted your partner pretty deeply, especially since they both live together and, in many ways, can't avoid one another. Moving out isn't currently an option for your partner, so this will be something they are coping with for a while.

You've had a discussion with your partner about your feelings and while they didn't seem upset about your feelings and gave their blessing for you to pursue the relationship, you can tell that they aren't in the best mental place now.

How do you handle this type of situation? What if the metamour wasn't interested in waiting for things to cool down? Or their separation had been more acrimonious, or they didn't live together? Consider different aspects of the situation and how it might affect your position.

SCENARIO 18: PAUSES

Many people respond to the problems and issues that they face within polyamory by deciding to close their relationship or pause other relationships to address what's going on. It makes logical sense on the surface, especially if the relationship began monogamously. If opening the relationship has caused the issues, then closing it makes sense.

Unfortunately, the issue that people often experience is that their problems exist within the structure of a non-monogamous relationship and they often need the structure to exist to solve those problems. This is similar to how some people think that they need to be single to fix themselves. I quite often remind people that there is no 'perfect' state that one can be in to be in a relationship.

Life doesn't care about how well you prepare for a relationship. Even if you could get to a 'perfect' state where you felt prepared for a relationship, life can throw you for a loop completely. Whether it's facing a death, job loss or anything else, there are no shortages of sudden crises that you may experience in life that can throw off any 'progress' you make with your mental health. 'Pausing' can make sense in some circumstances, but in others it might just be delaying the inevitable in terms of facing the issues that one must face in non-monogamy.

Situation

You're dating someone casually and they seem to be really struggling with their partner. At times they have requested pauses in your relationship with them. Since it has been casual, it hasn't been something that you've felt like was a huge problem for you; however, the anxiety of the situation is starting to affect you, especially as your relationship progresses.

At times, the details of the other relationship that your partner has given you have made you feel somewhat uncomfortable and now that you've considered it, you don't think it's fair to have your relationship put on pause.

How would you broach this subject with your partner? What sort of boundaries might you have around this situation and why? How might your approach change if you hadn't agreed to or had a pause before?

SCENARIO 19: FAMILY AND DISCLOSURE

The role of family within relationships is well established within monogamy. It's somewhat expected for partners to meet each other's families and that tends to be a big part of the cultural script of monogamy and deepening the relationship between two individuals. This can be difficult for people who don't have the best or any connection with their families.

Within polyamory, this can present some specific problems. Although a good deal of people know about 'open relationships', their perception is usually that open relationships are entirely focused on sex (which isn't necessarily an issue) or that they don't 'work'. Within the context of family, there are several reasons why people may feel awkward about being 'out' to their families about being non-monogamous.

Not every single person needs to be 'out' to their family about being non-monogamous. Deciding to not tell your family doesn't make you any less polyamorous or necessarily mean that you feel shame. You may decide you don't want to disclose to your family and instead choose to have one partner who meets your family and others who don't. I don't personally feel there is one right approach to this, but I can understand wanting to fit in with a new family or feeling the pressure to fit in.

Things to Consider

Work through the following questions on the theme of 'family and disclosure':

- Does your family know you are polyamorous or non-monogamous?
- Would you want to meet all your partners' families?
- How would you feel if your partner only allowed for one partner of theirs to meet their parents and you weren't that partner?
- Do you feel supported by your family in general? What obstacles do you feel there would be in introducing any of your partners to your family?

....

....

SCENARIO 20: RULES

You may have already heard people rail hard against rules to the point where they outrightly say that they have no rules. In the past, I have compared this to when people new to kink communities say they have no hard limits or anything that is completely off limits in the kinds of kink activities they are willing to try when they actually, definitely, do. However, there are some differences with regard to rules and how they work in non-monogamy.

I believe a lot of people make rules in polyamory in an attempt to control things, and that's not necessarily a terrible thing. For example, a lot of people make rules around requiring their partners to inform them before they get into a relationship or have sex with someone else. Very few people tend to realize how applying these rules may not work out the best for them, because they're thinking more about the fear of what will happen. A lot of people are very understandably scared of losing their partners, especially if they agreed to polyamory mainly to avoid a breakup.

What I encourage people to do is honestly come to terms with the fact that if the rules of monogamy cannot prevent people from losing their partners then no rule that they create will ultimately prevent their partner from leaving if it's something that they're going to do. We can be decent to our partners and put effort into the relationship, but we can't change whether our partners stay in love with us or not. However, when it comes to STIs, usually there are a lot of rules around exposure levels – because that is a little bit easier to control than feelings.

Things to Consider

Work through the following questions on the theme of 'rules':

- Do you have rules in mind, or have you enforced rules in relationships?
- Are you anti-rule in general?
- What would you change about how you implemented or will implement rules based on what you have learned?

. . . .

. . . .

Theme: Structure

SCENARIO 1: BUILDING FAMILIES

There are many ways to build families and not every single family needs to involve children, but when introducing children into the mix – whether that's future or current children – there are considerations that many people should think through that may not come up within a monogamous context.

I have witnessed a lack of discussion of how to balance childcare and home care when opening a relationship, especially where one partner wants to open the relationship and date and the other person has less of an interest in it.

To put it bluntly, I've seen many situations where someone is frequently stuck with the kids while their partner goes out on dates. In many cases, because the person stuck with the kids doesn't yet have another partner, their right to schedule time outside of the home alone or with friends gets deprioritized or ignored. It's important to think about some of the actual physical time and balance of domestic responsibilities when it comes to polyamory because when it does fall by the wayside, this often exacerbates the emotional difficulty that non-monogamy can already bring.

Things to Consider

Work through the following questions on the theme of 'building families':

- What do you see as the major positives and negatives of building a family in your current relationship structure?
- How might your relationship structure change if you added a child to the family?
- What is your current division, if it applies, of domestic responsibilities and do you feel like the division works best for you?
- What kind of family structure are you interested in?

....

....

....

....

SCENARIO 2: BREAKING UP

In all relationship styles, breaking up can come with a lot of social stigma as well as understandable feelings of lack or failure. We often define a 'successful' relationship as one that lasts for as long as possible. But logically, we know that there have been histories of long, unhappy marriages.

Within non-monogamy, there is also the additional aspect that many people feel pressure to prove they can 'do' non-monogamy. Especially when there are complications in a relationship, fearing that it could look like the relationship failed because you couldn't hack it can put pressure on you to stay in the relationship even when it doesn't serve you. And specifically, I've witnessed many people who are unsatisfied with their current partner try to open their relationship and find other partners, rather than just breaking up. Dating more than one person can also sometimes make it obvious when one relationship isn't working the same way others are.

Things to Consider

Work through the following questions on the theme of 'breaking up':

- What is the best way for someone to break up with you? What ways do you prefer to break up with others?
- Share your worst experience, if you have one, of initiating a breakup or receiving a breakup.
- What do you feel you have learned from breakups that you now employ in your current relationships?

....

....

....

....

....

....

....

SCENARIO 3: WORTH IT

It's rare for anyone to grow up knowing that polyamory is an option for them, and it's a little rarer for people to discover non-monogamy when they are not already in a relationship. While I can't say for sure what the actual ratio is of people who discover non-monogamy when they're single to those already in a relationship, I would say most people who come to me for help are often wanting to open an already existing relationship.

The question that a lot of people have, even before they approach their partners, is whether polyamory is 'worth it'. Introducing the idea that you would like to see other people can often spell the end of a monogamous relationship, so they may not want to ask this if they don't feel that polyamory is something they *need* to explore. Ultimately, this isn't something that I can always answer, because it depends on the individual.

Things to Consider

Work through the following questions on the theme of 'being worth it':

- What makes non-monogamy 'worth it' to you despite any challenges? Does this change throughout time or during different experiences?
- Would you risk a monogamous relationship to move into non-monogamy and why? Would that change depending on the length of the relationship?
- If you have a longer history of non-monogamy, when have you felt like things have been 'worth it' and when have you felt like things have not been 'worth it'?

....

....

....

....

....

....

SCENARIO 4: COHABITATION

There is the assumption in polyamory that partners who live together always prioritize each other, but I have said for a long while that I don't feel this is always the case. As aforementioned, living together doesn't mean spending quality time with one another.

When this is a polyamorous setup, it can be very easy to feel that other, newer partners get more dedicated quality time than you do, even if you live with your partner and are told by the polyamorous society around you that you are the partner who has the leverage and the power over others. Add to that the complications that living together can bring (such as arguing over laundry) and you have a recipe for feeling like you are the boring partner and everyone else just gets to have fun.

For many people, cohabitation is their only realistically economical option for being able to see their partners frequently. Very few people have the economic means to even have separate bedrooms in one house when living with a partner.

Things to Consider

Work through the following questions on the theme of 'cohabitation':

- How do you feel about living with romantic partners or the people you date?
- What aspects of cohabitation interest you – or don't interest you?
- What role does cohabitation play in your overall concept of 'relationship progression'?
- Do you feel there is a 'right time' to move into a cohabitation state?
- If you're interested in cohabitation, what are the downsides of it? If you're not interested in cohabitation, what are the upsides of it?

....

....

....

....

SCENARIO 5: YOUR ANCHOR

One of the concepts I have introduced is the 'anchor', which is a personal, individual reason that someone has that motivates them to try polyamory or non-monogamy. I encourage people to find this anchor because, especially when non-monogamy becomes difficult, looking back to the personal reasons why you've decided to pursue this can be a grounding exercise against what I feel are the typical and understandable anxieties most people will have in non-monogamy.

I strongly encourage people to have an anchor which is not based around saving an existing relationship or avoiding a breakup. This is because when people do this, the relationship they want to 'save' is a monogamous one where nothing about their life with their partner changes and on a basic level that relationship no longer exists. While it is no doubt a benefit to not have to end a relationship, one must come to terms with the fact that the structure and day to day of their relationship has fundamentally changed.

People who are monogamous to a non-monogamous person can still have an anchor. Your reason for being interested in polyamory may be because you're an independent person who likes your alone time, and traditional monogamy would often mean feeling pressured to spend more time than you want to with a romantic partner. It doesn't always have to be that you have a burning interest to date others or even establish more than one other new relationship. But if you can find a reason for why you, as an individual, are interested in non-monogamy, you can easily remind yourself of that reason when it gets hard, in the same way you can remind yourself of your end goal of, for example, graduating with a diploma, when you're struggling to write an essay or missing an opportunity to go out with friends or party because you need to study.

Things to Consider

Work through the following questions on the theme of 'your anchor':

- What was your introduction into polyamory or non-monogamy?
- What messages do you feel you have received from the society you grew up in and in your home life about monogamy that have influenced how you perceived non-monogamy?

- What personal, individualized reason do you have for wanting to be non-monogamous or to try a non-monogamous relationship?
- What are the benefits for your life you can see in being in a non-monogamous relationship?
- What are the negatives for your life you can see in being in a non-monogamous relationship?

SCENARIO 6: LABELS

Labels are best when treated as devices for communicating or for understanding oneself rather than a prescriptive list of expectations people need to meet. Throughout the years, I have gone from identifying as 'polyamorous' to 'non-monogamous' to now not seeing my relationship style as a critical part of who I am or something that takes up an especially large space in terms of my identity.

For some people, defining themselves as 'polyamorous' highlights the important aspect that having multiple *romantic* relationships has in their lives (vs. the idea that 'non-monogamy' may mean that you have one central romantic relationship and other sexual relationships), and others prefer the term 'multiamorous' because they dislike the mix of Greek (*poly*) and Latin (*amor*). There have also been discussions about the use of 'poly' as a shorthand because 'Poly' is often used as a shorthand for Polynesian, making it difficult for Polynesian people to find their communities online.

Not all definitions are the same, and because this is a developing concept, the language around it can be constantly changing, but it might be helpful to figure out what the role of these labels have in your life and personal expression.

Things to Consider

Work through the following questions on the theme of 'labels':

- How do you define yourself? Polyamorous? Non-monogamous?
- Is there a specific reason you have chosen a specific word?
- What do you feel are the main differences between these terms: polyamorous, non-monogamous, ethically non-monogamous, open? Do those differences matter to you?
- What role does your relationship style play in your personal identity?

....

....

....

SCENARIO 7: RELATIONSHIP MILESTONES

The monogamous cultural script many of the scenarios in this book refer to has a strong influence on our social construction of relationships and the role we view them playing in our lives. Over the years, this social script has very much changed. Whereas in the past, monogamous heterosexual marriage along with children would have been expected for all, there are wider views today of different ways to live.

Despite these changes, many still feel a certain pressure within relationships to hit certain milestones: dating, becoming romantically/sexually exclusive, establishing their relationship in public, anniversaries, meeting parents or family, living together, buying shared assets together, and having children or other types of responsibilities. Depending on where you live, these milestones may still be heavy cultural expectations even if modern attitudes might be less stringent. They often represent a 'deeper' level of commitment and one of the biggest confounding experiences many people have in non-monogamy is how to define what 'progression' means within an atypical relationship style.

Because emotional intimacy isn't easily measurable and differs from person to person, socially we often rely on these 'milestones' to demonstrate our closeness to others. And in a relationship where you may choose to move in with only one partner or none, defining these milestones in all of your relationships can be somewhat tricky. And not everyone has an interest in any of these milestones.

Situation

You begin dating someone new and, as you typically do, after a couple of dates when you feel as though you would like to make things more 'official', you initiate a discussion about where your partner feels the relationship between you may 'progress' or what kind of milestones are important to you. In this example, many of the typical cultural milestones of relationships such as moving in together or meeting parents are both available and of interest to you.

The person you're dating, however, has an extreme aversion to defining any aspect of your relationship in an 'official' capacity and has no set milestones or plans for anything. They are very hesitant to set anything in stone in terms of plans or official definitions. They aren't necessarily against the ideas of, for example, moving in together or meeting parents, but they have no wish to make that into 'a thing'.

How would you deal with this situation? If you are more like the other partner, how would you deal with a request for more definition in your relationship where you do not have a desire for it?

SCENARIO 8: RESTRICTED PROGRESS

For most people, it is difficult to put our finger on exactly when we feel 'more' for someone, and it can be difficult to even describe how our feelings work in any objective way. We quite often don't have control over when our feelings grow deeper, which further adds complication to situations where we might be restricted in how far the relationship may be able to go.

There may be a variety of reasons why a relationship may remain 'casual' and I tend to find when giving advice that the difficulty with these types of situations tends to be when the boundaries are not communicated and one person has the expectation that a relationship will grow 'deeper' when the other person does not. Where something is overtly communicated, that may be somewhat safer, but it doesn't mean you can control how your feelings grow.

Situation

After a few dates with someone you have a lot of interest in, they let you know that they are also interested, but they do not have the time and space for very much in their life now so they feel like your relationship together would be more along the lines of a 'friends with benefits' style of a relationship than a full-on romantic relationship.

Overall, you feel really pulled to continue meeting up with this person and struggle to know truly if you might develop any deeper feelings further down the line. You've never been in this type of situation before where you knew ahead of time that the relationship couldn't 'progress' the way it usually would. You have, however, been in situations where a partner hasn't set this boundary but it's happened anyway, and it was super painful.

How do you deal with this type of situation and risk? Are you averse to trying this type of situation or are you comfortable with it? How might your reaction to this situation change if you had no other partners at the time or were going through a particularly difficult period in your life?

. . . .

. . . .

. . . .

SCENARIO 9: OPEN AND SHUT

Many monogamous people can feel comfortable being monogamous to a polyamorous person, for a variety of reasons. However, some polyamorous people may feel uncomfortable with the idea of a partner being monogamous to them, even if it's by choice, because they feel uncomfortable with the idea that their partner is restricted and they are not.

I have seen a few cases where someone who was monogamous to a polyamorous person ended up changing their mind and becoming interested in a polyamorous relationship later. Even when the polyamorous partner may not have any logical objections, the shift in the relationship can still cause some understandable trepidation. Quite often changes in relationship structures or definitions can elicit worries, even when they are welcome.

Situation

You have a partner who decided they wanted to be monogamous to you or weren't very interested in dating other people. They weren't actively pursuing other people for a while and after a period, they wanted to make it 'official' that they were only dating you.

By 'official', they want to not say they're in an 'open' relationship on social media profiles, and to close all their dating profiles, introduce you to their family as their only partner and bring you to most of the functions that involve taking a partner. On occasion, they may hide the fact that you are non-monogamous. This makes you slightly anxious but you're okay with that.

After a few months, your partner meets someone at work and wants to change their mind about being monogamous, specifically to date that person. This sudden switch isn't theoretically a problem for you. After all, you felt a little bit unsure about them deciding to be monogamous, but this was what you least expected.

How would you handle this situation? Would you date someone who wanted to be monogamous to you? Would you object to being presented to someone as a monogamous pair, either explicitly or through implicit assumption? Before agreeing to a relationship where someone is monogamous to you, what aspects of the relationship do you think would be important to discuss? If you are monogamous to someone who is polyamorous, what interests you about the situation?

SCENARIO 10: QUICK PROGRESSION

There is no one correct speed at which a relationship should 'progress' – however one defines progression. Typically, the definition of 'progression', especially in non-monogamy, involves spending more and more time with another partner. There is no one right way for things to progress or one speed that things need to develop in and it comes down to the individuals.

When you have defined the physical aspects of how you want to spend your time in polyamory, there is a lot less concern about the 'progression' of relationships. Spending scheduled time together as well as spending time you would use to go out on dates apart can help make it easier when you do actually date.

When the physical aspects go undefined, I have seen many situations where people end up getting caught in what's called 'new relationship energy' or the honeymoon phase of a new relationship and sometimes forget to schedule time with their other partners, especially when people are living together. From that perspective, it then seems like the new relationship is progressing 'too quickly'.

Things to Consider

Work through the following questions on the theme of 'quick progression':

- What defines a relationship progression to you? Does it involve time spent?
- How do you feel about your partner's other relationships progressing 'quickly'?
- How would you cope with the anxiety you might have around your partner's relationship progression?

....

....

....

....

....

SCENARIO 11: INHERENTLY POLYAMOROUS

No one can really tell you if polyamory is 'for you' or not. Some people feel that polyamory isn't just a choice for them but inherently a part of who they are, so they may never have the experience of wondering if it is 'worth it'.

All too often, I feel, many polyamory resources are quick to label people who are feeling emotional or struggling with things like jealousy as not truly 'polyamorous', or insist that there might be something wrong with someone who doesn't identify closely with polyamory. Struggling with strong emotions doesn't necessarily mean that polyamory is not 'for you'. And I do find that even those who closely identify with being polyamorous still sometimes experience some negativity, fear and other emotions they never thought they would when they first tried polyamory.

Whether or not you're inherently polyamorous and what that means is difficult to clearly define. This can be similar to the discussion of whether or not polyamory is 'worth it', but more specific to your inherent personal identity.

Things to Consider

Work through the following questions on the theme of being 'inherently polyamorous':

- Do you feel you are inherently polyamorous?
- How do you think you might know if you stop feeling polyamorous or stop wanting polyamory?
- What signs have you had to show that polyamory is 'for you', or what do you expect to feel or see?

....

....

....

....

....

....

SCENARIO 12: LONG DISTANCE

At times, people can use non-monogamy to avoid breaking up with people, and this can especially be the case when it comes to long distance. I don't think it's always a bad thing to want to avoid breaking up with your partner, but it's important not to maintain several unsatisfactory relationships just to avoid breaking up.

Long-distance relationships come with a lot of specific challenges which some people don't really want to engage with, understandably. Adding polyamory to the mix can also cause strong, difficult emotions when you can't see your partner but someone else can. If there's ever a situation where I absolutely do think that people are feeling jealousy for a very understandable reason, it's in a long-distance relationship when a metamour has access to a partner that you don't, and there's not necessarily much that can be done to counteract that.

It's important to both acknowledge the specific challenges that long distance will bring and to plan for strategies to tackle those challenges. Setting time aside to address this is one of the crucial aspects that help make these situations a little more manageable.

Situation

You have a partner that you live with or see extremely frequently, and you both have plans to buy a house together.

Suddenly, your partner is offered a work opportunity, but it means they will be gone for three months and it's very unlikely that you'll be able to see them throughout these three months. You're happy for your partner but have struggled with long distance in the past.

How would you feel in this situation? What if the period was a bit longer than three months – six months? A year? And how might not having made any plans with this partner change how you feel or how you manage this situation? How might the situation change if you could do long distance easily?

....

....

SCENARIO 13: ASKING TO OPEN UP

Introducing the concept of non-monogamy into a monogamous relationship is a situation many people find themselves in. While I do encourage people to jump into the deep end rather than 'easing' themselves into polyamory (because 'easing' often involves unrealistic rules), jumping into the deep end by asking your partner about it is a whole other ballgame.

One of the things I suggest to people who are a little anxious about introducing the topic to their partner is to begin with the concept of the 'hall pass' and see how their partner reacts to it. If you're unfamiliar, a 'hall pass' is a list of one or more people, usually celebrities, that your partner has a free pass to sleep with if they ever have the chance. A partner who finds the idea of you being able to sleep with other people in a hypothetical scenario repulsive probably won't react positively to the concept of non-monogamy or opening a relationship.

There are other ways, if you are only interested in the sexual aspects of exploring other relationships, to open up. Exploring things like going out to swingers clubs, hiring a sex worker if that is something you can do where you live, or what's known as monogamous group sex (or MGS – 'megs') where you have sex in front of other couples without swapping can all be ways that you can explore other sexual opportunities without fully 'opening'.

Things to Consider

Work through the following questions on the theme of 'opening up':

- Have you been the one to ask a partner to open your relationship or become polyamorous, have you been the one asked, or both?
- What was your initial reaction either way? What was the result?
- How might you do it differently if you could do it all over again?

....

....

....

....

SCENARIO 14: SATISFYING RELATIONSHIPS

I frequently remind people that polyamory is not an excuse to stay in multiple unsatisfying relationships and that the approach that 'one person can't meet all your needs' can encourage people to see others as need-fulfilling machines in a way that I don't think is extremely helpful.

But what makes a relationship 'satisfying'? Sometimes we have an unrealistic expectation of relationship happiness, especially when we're comparing our day to day with someone's highlight reel on social media. Relationships also are not always perfectly 50/50 and sometimes do require some compromise and work. Expecting a relationship to always be 100 per cent satisfying is unrealistic. Life happens and different types of events happen that cause us to need others more and need more support.

Add that to the fact that if you're new to polyamory, you might struggle with a lot of overwhelming emotions, it makes sense that your relationship may not feel particularly satisfying in the moments when you're struggling. Specifically, I remember thinking that I was extremely polyamorous because I felt very lonely in a relationship and had a huge drive to find another relationship, when actually the issue was the relationship I was in.

Things to Consider

Work through the following questions on the theme of 'satisfying relationships':

- What makes a relationship satisfying to you?
- When does a relationship become something that enriches your life – or something that doesn't?
- Have you experienced that shift in any relationship you've been in, monogamous or otherwise?
- How does polyamory affect your perception of a 'satisfying relationship'?

....

....

....

SCENARIO 15: MEETING METAMOURS

Although there is no 'one way' to do polyamory, a lot of people understandably want to get along with their metamours. While I totally understand this and have felt the pressure to do so myself, I have also put so much pressure on myself to meet and 'get along' with metamours that I've made myself more uncomfortable than I needed to be in those situations.

My first experience of polyamory involved being used to cheat, so I initially had a rule that I had to meet all my metamours but then eventually, after forcing myself to be in friendships with metamours that didn't work well, I loosened up my requirements a little and I realized I had to trust my partners. Now, I have much looser requirements around this and don't even necessarily have to meet my metamours.

People can feel trepidation around meeting their metamours or, equally, not meeting their metamours. If someone doesn't want to meet them, some people consider that to be a red flag.

Situation

It's important for you to be on good terms with your metamours and it's never been something you've had an issue with before. But now your partner is dating someone who has specifically requested to not be forced to meet up with you. While you didn't have any intention of forcing your metamour to meet up with you, the fact that they don't want to meet up with you is causing you a lot more anxiety than you anticipated.

There is no timeline as to when this request will expire or no specific date which you might meet. Your shared partner seems comfortable with your metamour's boundaries and doesn't see any kind of issue with it.

Would you feel anxious in this situation and how might you manage it? Would you only agree with this if there was a specific timeframe? Would it change if you lived or didn't live with your partner? What kind of discussions might you have with your partner about this – if at all?

. . . .

. . . .

. . . .

SCENARIO 16: MANAGING METAMOURS

Shared living spaces are a challenge for many. Having to negotiate your space with other people can be frustrating and difficult. If you add polyamory to that situation, it can create even more awkwardness.

As much as it might be nice for everyone to be able to have their own room and their own space, realistically a lot of people are struggling to find enough space for themselves. There are running jokes about polyamory being a secret plot to get cheaper housing, and that's understandable. For much of one of my longer relationships, we lived in shared housing where there wasn't even a living room, let alone space for us to have partners over.

Whenever that situation arises, navigating space can be difficult. Getting a hotel is not always a suitable option for privacy and not everyone has friends they can stay with at the drop of a hat when someone else wants privacy. The result is that interacting with metamours may be something that happens fairly frequently.

Situation

You and a partner you don't live with have been together for a while. You both have your own space but it is in shared accommodation. You're frequently visiting one another in your own spaces.

They begin dating someone new who is either living with them or who shares some of the same spaces and visits as often as you do. You're not necessarily practising a parallel form of polyamory, where people keep their relationships separate but not necessarily hidden from one another, but the metamour doesn't seem to be that interested in communicating with you much, which makes visiting your partner when they're around a little bit more awkward than it would be if they were a little more friendly.

How do you manage this type of situation? Would it be different if it was someone your partner lived with compared to someone who was visiting frequently? Do you feel like you should address the situation or is it for your shared partner to address?

. . . .

. . . .

SCENARIO 17: PREVIOUS EXPERIENCE

A lot of people spend a good number of years as they grow up thinking about their ideal monogamous relationship, and quite often people don't really have the same imaginative space when they start out in non-monogamy. The issue can be, as many people will have experienced with monogamy, that you sometimes don't realize what you want until you've had experience within a relationship. Or that you think you want something until you actually have it.

Even if you haven't had experience within polyamorous relationships, the experience you have outside of that can still be valuable. If you're new to all types of romantic relationships, then the application of what you've experienced within friendships could still be helpful, and there's nothing wrong in having different experiences and learning what it is that you like within relationships.

Because a lot of people have a lot of shame around the concept of breaking up, it's sometimes difficult to see the idea of going through several different types of relationships to figure out what you want as a positive thing, but the more you figure out what you want, the easier it can be to find it.

Things to Consider

Work through the following questions on the theme of 'previous experience':

- Is there a specific relationship you have had that really helped you realize what you want from relationships?
- Is there a specific relationship or experience you have had that helped you realize what you don't want from relationships?
- What else has helped you figure out what you do and don't want out of relationships?

. . . .

. . . .

. . . .

. . . .

SCENARIO 18: BELIEVING IN MONOGAMY

Many people believe that monogamy doesn't 'work' for a lot of different reasons. Should we assume monogamy doesn't work purely because of the divorce rate when people used to stay together because they had no other choice and now, in many parts of the world, no longer have to? Should we assume that a relationship that doesn't last for the rest of your lifetime hasn't 'worked' for you?

Some people feel that monogamy inherently doesn't work for them – and that's valid! But I have always felt that assuming monogamy doesn't work for anybody is ridiculous given the vast number of people on the planet, the diversity of experiences, and the fact that there are monogamous people who have been monogamous their entire lives.

Things to Consider

Work through the following questions on the theme of 'believing in monogamy':

- Do you believe that monogamy doesn't 'work'?
- Would you date someone who believed monogamy didn't 'work'?

....

....

....

....

....

....

....

....

....

....

Theme: Emotions

SCENARIO 1: RESURFACING EMOTIONS

All new relationships can bring up wounds from previous relationships. While this is sometimes seen as 'baggage', this is pretty normal for most people. Throughout my time giving advice, I've seen a lot of people willing to define themselves as broken because they have 'hang-ups' from previous relationships. We can't always control the wounds we have from previous relationships, but we can be aware of them and how they affect our actions.

If we have not been polyamorous in the past, there are aspects of polyamory that might bring up some things we don't expect, because it's a different approach and lifestyle, and it doesn't have the same cultural backing and script as monogamy does. If we have had previous polyamorous relationships, then there may be wounds from those that end up surfacing.

Someone once said, 'Between stimulus and response there is a space. In that space is our power to choose our response. In our response lies our growth and our freedom.' I often use this quote, and didn't at first realize that it had been incorrectly attributed to Austrian psychologist and Holocaust survivor Viktor Frankl, according to the Viktor Frankl Institute.[1] This is one of the perspectives that helped me overcome anxiety. A lot of online cultures, in my opinion, encourage people to believe we cannot choose our response and that this space between stimulus and response doesn't exist. I think it is better to step into your own power of choice. We can't choose our wounds, but we can choose our response.

Things to Consider

Work through the following questions on the theme of 'resurfacing emotions':

- What wounds from previous relationships do you see cropping up in your current relationships?
- How do you address those wounds or prepare for them showing up?
- In what way does polyamory or non-monogamy trigger some of your wounds in particular?
- What strategies could you put in place to address the resurfacing of these emotions?

1 www.viktorfrankl.org/quote_stimulus.html

SCENARIO 2: TRUST IMBALANCE

Quite often I tell people to expect the worst when it comes to their emotions, especially on the first night their partner is on a date or away with someone else. This isn't to say that it will always be terrible, but if you expect the worst, you can prepare yourself. And this also isn't to say that the second night might be better, but my experience is usually that over time, you feel less and less anxious, especially as the experience of your partner being out becomes more normal.

However, the anxiety decreasing over time isn't necessarily assured. In which case, there might be something else going on that's encouraging the anxiety or deeper issues that might be causing the anxiety. Not feeling like your relationship has a stable ground can be normal if you haven't had the foundational discussions about the role polyamory plays in your life and how you envision your partner being part of your future.

Likewise, if you're in a relationship where your partner doesn't spend quality time with you and that's important to you, then spending time with other people, especially doing things you wish you were doing with your partner, is naturally going to trigger a lot of anxiety. There are any number of reasons why the anxiety might not decrease over time.

Situation

You and your partner have been polyamorous for a few months (either you started as polyamorous or became so). Both of you have gone on dates and overnights with other people, and each time you've had a date or an overnight, your partner hasn't shown any sign of anxiety or worry. They've never needed any reassurance or seemed to have any sort of problem.

However, you're finding that every time your partner has a date, you're swimming with anxiety to the point where it's almost unbearable. You've struggled to reconcile why this is and have not told your partner about your feelings.

What would you do in this situation as the partner feeling a lot of anxiety? What would you do as the person whose partner is feeling a lot of anxiety? What solutions do you think you could brainstorm together to address this problem?

SCENARIO 3: CHEMISTRY

One of the things we're taught within a monogamous-centric society is that if we have chemistry or an attraction to someone, it's something that must be pursued and developed into a relationship. When a crush or attraction doesn't eventually end up in a relationship, then it's seen as a 'loss' in some way. This is further reinforced by ideas like the 'friend zone' or that if you don't develop a relationship, you are 'just friends'.

Often, I have asked people to explore the idea that they could enjoy the feeling of having an attraction to someone without the need for that to be pursued into something. As I've said before, contrary to assumptions, becoming polyamorous doesn't necessarily widen your dating pool. And there may be many situations where you find yourself attracted to someone and they have no interest in polyamory.

Or, conversely, some people want to introduce the concept of polyamory to their relationships because they are attracted to someone else and feel like there must be some 'result' from the chemistry. There are a lot more possibilities available to people than they sometimes think.

Things to Consider

Work through the following questions on the theme of 'chemistry':

- What is your relationship to chemistry and experiencing it with others? Does it happen frequently or rarely?
- How does chemistry change as your relationships with people develop?
- Have you felt like you needed to act upon your chemistry?
- What are some situations where you haven't been able to act on chemistry and how did those situations develop, or not?

....

....

....

....

SCENARIO 4: DEVELOPING FEELINGS

When partners open their relationship, they often agree on a rule that they won't fall in love with anyone else, or that they will let their partner know when a relationship 'develops into something more'. There are any number of variants on these rules. Rules may aim to prevent 'more' from happening between other people, or to create some type of early warning system for the other partner.

Usually this isn't done out of a desire to control someone (and both people may agree happily to these rules), but is instead done to manage the fear of losing their partner or being replaced. What I encourage people to consider, rather than leaning on these rules, is that if the exclusivity rule of monogamy doesn't prevent people from losing their partners or being replaced, why would any of these types of rules do that in an open relationship?

It's also not necessarily easy for someone to pinpoint when a relationship becomes 'more', when they fall in love, or when they start to want something more 'serious' from someone else. Realistically, what people often want to be prepared for are changes in their relationship with their partner. If you discuss how you will manage your time beforehand and begin spending time apart, that will work far better than these 'heads up' rules often do. Still, it might be important to explore with each other where the lines are.

Things to Consider

Work through the following questions on the theme of 'developing feelings':

- How do you know when you are 'developing feelings' for someone?
- What typically happens when you have 'feelings' for someone that are different from friendships?
- How do relationships differ from friendships to you?
- Do you have a 'friends with benefits' type of category that feels different?
- What does it mean to you when you 'develop feelings'?

. . . .

. . . .

SCENARIO 5: BAD REPUTATION

Even in the most parallel of polyamories, many of us would reasonably care about what our metamours think of us to a certain extent, just as we would reasonably care about what our partner's family and friends think of us. Even in situations where metamours don't meet, other relationships may impact us in ways that can't always be avoided. To define the term, 'parallel polyamory' is a style of polyamory where partners keep their relationships separate but not necessarily hidden from one another so that they happen in parallel.

In many cases, I encourage people to avoid making judgements and assumptions about metamours, especially because it's very easy for one to blame a metamour for decisions that a partner has made. It's also difficult to make judgements and assumptions about relationships that you're not involved in when you only hear one side of all the information.

We also are all human, and we make mistakes. Within polyamory, where we're dealing with new situations we've never encountered before we're even more likely to make mistakes. When emotions are running high, it's also a lot easier to say things you don't mean or do things you wouldn't typically do. In those cases, we may not be the best version of ourselves and may not make the best impression on others in ways that are difficult to rectify.

Situation

You recently struggled with an intense bout of anxiety and one of your partners cancelled a date with one of your metamours to help you through it. It was difficult but you are feeling a lot better and don't foresee this becoming an issue again. Your partner has told you now though that your metamour has been expressing concern about the relationship you and your partner have. Your metamour has described you as 'controlling' and even suggested the relationship you have with your partner is 'abusive'.

Your metamour has only expressed this so far to your shared partner, but the polyamory community where you live is very small and there are a lot of shared connections and friends between all three of you. Your partner doesn't seem influenced by this and hasn't really mentioned how or if they plan to respond.

How would you handle this situation? Would it change if it was your metamour who felt you were being abused by your partner instead?

SCENARIO 6: DISCUSSING EMOTIONS

Whenever we're going through difficult emotions, it's common for a lot of people to ignore their own feelings. Psychologist Gabor Maté discusses frequently how it's common in our culture for children to be encouraged to suppress their own emotions. Many of the ways we raise children encourage them to choose between their authentic selves and remaining attached to their caregivers – and this is without the added experience of additional trauma.

Add that to the complication that polyamory often feels like something someone should have to prove that they can do. Most people, if they do know about 'open relationships', have heard that or strongly believe that that they 'don't work', which results in a large amount of pressure on people both culturally and individually to 'prove' they can 'do polyamory' and the result of that is often that when people feel strong emotions, they don't express them.

Likewise, though I do advocate that we control our responses to things in life, a lot of people take this to mean that emotions should be supressed, ignored and definitely not expressed to anyone, which is not what I mean. There are going to be many times, even within monogamy, where people struggle to express feeling jealous, violated, worried, anxious or more to their partner, and sometimes hearing a partner say they haven't been happy when you think they have can bring up guilt, confusion and frustration.

Situation

After returning from a date with another person, you wished to show your partner that you were still interested in them as a means of reassurance. You did this by initiating something sexual when you got home, but your partner wasn't interested. You didn't really take this personally at the time or think much of it.

A few weeks later, your partner brings up the incident and says they felt upset about what happened. They felt like your sexual interest in them was a result of being on a date with someone else but not being able to go home with them, which made them feel self-conscious about their body and attractiveness. Since that incident, there have been a few more times when something similar happened and you feel frustrated that they waited so long to tell you.

How would you handle this situation? Do you feel similar feelings if you find out that something you've done has not made your partner feel great? What does that bring up for you? How do you handle situations where you don't feel great, and you don't bring it up in the moment but have to address it later?

SCENARIO 7: PRIORITY REASSURANCE

Especially when people begin a relationship monogamously and open it up, it's common for one of them to attempt to reassure their partner by saying things like 'You're the most important person to me,' or even openly admit that they will not be as in love with others as they are with their partner. It's understandable. That's often how we comfort our partners in monogamous situations when they're scared that we're attracted to someone else.

When people have an agreement that other relationships outside of the 'the couple' are more like friends with benefits and everyone (including people outside 'the couple') is aware of this, I don't think this method of reassurance is necessarily a problem.

However, even if you decide to have a 'primary' partner, I don't feel this is always the best approach to take, because if there is one position of 'top partner' and that is a position that can be lost, then you have a lot to lose. It is one more thing to worry about within a lot of other things to worry about. Even though the idea is to be comforting, reaffirming that there is only one 'top' position may cause more worry later down the line than it solves.

Additionally, as much as we may believe that we will always feel the same about our partner, that isn't something that is within our control, so isn't something we can guarantee. Obviously, we can choose to feed our relationships and give them the care they need, or we can ignore them, but we can't always control our feelings.

Situation

You occasionally find yourself a little anxious when your partner goes out on dates. One of the main ways that your partner reassures you is by saying that you are the most important relationship that they have, that they will always love you more than anyone else, and that no one else compares to you.

How does this type of reassurance make you feel? In what way would you respond to this type of reassurance? If your partner wanted this type of reassurance, how would you respond?

SCENARIO 8: CONFLICT MANAGEMENT

A lot of people have been told 'don't go to bed angry' when it comes to relationships. There are a lot of reasons why this isn't very good advice – after all, we're not at our best when we're exhausted. It's something that I've also really struggled with. I find it difficult/impossible to sleep when I feel agitated from an argument, but now, I feel sorry for the partners I have kept up late into the night with impossible discussions that would have been better left until we both had some adequate rest.

Some people, especially those who have had to walk on eggshells in relationships or when they were growing up, might feel that conflict in their relationship is a 'risk'. For a very long time, I saw my relationships as these perfect stones that got chipped away with every argument, and had to re-conceptualize my thought process. I had to realize that conflict not only was an inevitable part of a relationship but also that it sometimes brought us closer together.

Things to Consider

Work through the following questions on the theme of 'conflict management':

- How do you handle conflict overall in your relationships?
- What did you learn about conflict growing up, and how does that affect you today?
- What role do you feel conflict plays in relationships, especially in polyamory?
- Can you think of a time when you handled conflict poorly and how you might have done it differently?
- Can you think of a time when you handled conflict well? What helped you make it more successful?

. . . .

. . . .

. . . .

. . . .

SCENARIO 9: COMPARISONS

People very much struggle with comparisons to others even in monogamy. It's difficult for us to step back from comparing ourselves to others, especially because we're encouraged through consumerism to believe it's best to always be in competition with others, and of course that consuming is how we better ourselves or make ourselves stand out.

Within monogamy, there is a very easy way of counteracting this. In monogamy, your partner is with you and only you. But with polyamory, there can be more of an 'active' threat because your partner is also sleeping with someone else. There is an active chance to compare someone directly, whereas in monogamy you may forget previous partners or others who found your partner attractive at any point.

It's difficult not to let your mind wonder about how you compare to other people. Likewise, unfortunately, we can find ourselves comparing our partners to each other, especially in terms of their different ways of supporting us, or different ways they show up in our relationships. And very few people want to have to ask one partner to be more like another.

Things to Consider

Work through the following questions on the theme of 'comparisons':

- Do you struggle to not compare yourselves to others in terms of relationships or anything else in life?
- What is your relationship to the fear of being replaced? How does it show up for you?
- How would you address a situation where you found yourself comparing one partner to another?
- Do you think there is a difference between how frequently or the ways in which you compare yourself to others in polyamory as opposed to monogamy?

....

....

....

SCENARIO 10: WANTING TO GO BACK

In addition to difficulties within relationships, polyamory can also be challenging when you're faced with a situation where you're more than ready to find another partner but, for whatever reason, you're not finding anyone available to date. Quite often, I see situations where one individual within a couple that has opened their relationship struggles to find a new partner and the other doesn't, but finding new partners can be difficult for anyone.

As much as people may joke about non-monogamy being for 'greedy' people in the same way that they do about bisexuality, the pool of people to choose from who are either already non-monogamous or who are interested in non-monogamy is small. If you're in a small town, the pool may be even smaller or non-existent. Even if you are in a larger city, people's willingness or ability to travel may be minimal, so most of your relationships may end up being long distance or you may not be able to see your partners very often.

Not everyone feels that non-monogamy is something that they identify with or that they *must* be non-monogamous, so there may not be a big reason for people to stay non-monogamous if they feel like they're not getting the *full* non-monogamous experience. So, for that reason, many people consider going back to monogamy.

Things to Consider

Work through the following questions on the theme of 'wanting to go back':

- Outside of the heat of emotional difficulties, have you ever wanted to 'go back' to monogamy?
- Would you consider going back to monogamy if you were single? And if you're single, what would make you consider going back to monogamy?

....

....

....

....

SCENARIO 11: RELATIONSHIP SUCCESS

A lot of people say monogamy doesn't 'work' because half of all marriages end in divorce – which is a statistic that a lot of polyamorous people quote when pointing out the hypocrisy of people believing that non-monogamy doesn't 'work'. But the issue hiding behind quoting this statistic is the assumption that a relationship is only successful if it lasts for the rest of your life.

While there isn't necessarily anything wrong with wanting to have a long-term relationship or celebrating longer anniversaries, the assumption that a relationship has to last a long time in order to be a 'success' or that any relationship that doesn't last until death is a 'failure' puts undue pressure on staying together. Because non-monogamy is already seen by many as doomed to failure, there is added pressure on polyamorous people not only to maintain relationships so as not to be seen as a failure, but also to prove through long-term relationships that polyamory 'works'.

There are a lot of different ways to define what makes a 'successful' relationship and it doesn't always have to include the relationship lasting for a very long time. One of my more successful relationships only lasted for a few months, but it had an enormous impact on me. If we're redefining the concept of relationships in terms of exclusivity, we should consider redefining whether they have to last for an extremely long time to be 'successful'.

Things to Consider

Work through the following questions on the theme of 'relationship success':

- How do you define 'success' in your relationships?
- What was your most 'successful' relationship? What was your least 'successful' relationship?
- Do you feel a pressure to prove polyamory 'works' through the longevity of your relationships?
- How does the pressure impact your relationships?

....

....

SCENARIO 12: EMOTIONAL PROCESSING

There is an ongoing joke about how much polyamorous people like to talk and have discussions about their relationships. There can be a lot of talking and working through certain things in non-monogamy. This isn't to say that monogamy doesn't involve a lot of processing, but because monogamy is part of our overall cultural script, people often don't end up talking a lot about different aspects of monogamy – even when they should!

However, there is such a thing as too much emotional processing, and at times it can be incredibly difficult to work through, especially if it feels like your emotional processing isn't really getting to any reliable solutions, or that you're just re-working the same issue over and over again. A lot of people struggle in relationships if they are very verbal processors of their emotions, and their partners are not. Not everyone needs to process their emotions through discussions, and some may prefer to work through their emotions in other ways. In polyamorous situations, where we're often hypervigilant about the status of our relationships, partners who tend to process internally can trigger anxiety in other partners.

Situation

You've been with a partner for a couple of years, and they tend to be attracted to people more frequently than you are. However, every time you are attracted to someone new, it involves a lot of long discussions with your partner that you often find incredibly draining, and there have been times where you have considered not pursuing the relationship because of the inevitable discussion.

What would you do in this situation, or have you felt exhausted by emotional processing in a relationship? How do you handle these types of situations? How do you process your emotions in your relationship? What kind of boundaries could you put in place if you struggled to help process emotions verbally?

....

....

....

SCENARIO 13: THE FIRST NIGHT

Whether you open a relationship from a monogamous one or begin a non-monogamous relationship, there is talking about polyamory and then there is practising it. The first time your partner spends the night with another person is where the rubber often meets the road, as I say. Personally, I have found that even if you are 'experienced', it can be a time of some trepidation and nerve-wracking feelings.

Quite often I remind people that, even if they were together for years before opening up their relationship, whenever you're starting off in polyamory, you're starting a new foundation of trust together, and if you're just starting in a new relationship that was polyamorous from the beginning, you're still building your foundation with one another. It makes sense to be anxious, even if you have 'chosen' or even identify with polyamory.

I encourage people to expect the worst when it comes to the first night a partner is away, either on a date or overnight. This may seem a little pessimistic or dramatic, but I find it's a little easier to expect the worst and prepare for it. Sometimes people can find a friend to hang out with during this time, or they may find it helpful to take themselves out on a date. During one of my relationships, I felt a lot better if I wrote cards for my partner and thought about what I was grateful for in our relationship.

Things to Consider

Work through the following questions on the theme of 'the first night':

- Have you been through this experience yet? How did it feel? Did you have the experience that you thought you would have?
- If you could re-do your experience, how would you have done it differently?
- If you haven't had this experience, what do you think you might feel? What do you think you could do to prepare for the first night?

....

....

....

SCENARIO 14: REGRET

The decision to pursue polyamory or open a relationship is a life-changing one, because, as much as I'm not a fan of the word 'lifestyle', polyamory is a different way of living. Many people don't really know if polyamory is for them until they try it, which is similar to a lot of other lifestyle decisions. Mixed feelings don't always necessarily reflect a bad decision.

One of the biggest reasons that it's hard for me to tell someone if polyamory will be 'worth it' for them or if it's going to be a regret for them is that there are a lot of complicated feelings that come with non-monogamy. Truthfully, there are a lot of complicated feelings that come with monogamy, but in monogamy we have a cultural script that helps us prepare for some of those feelings. Also, most of us go through our first relationships when we're younger, and it's easy to forget how stressful our first relationships were.

It can be difficult when you're confronting and changing your mind about some of the things a monogamous-centric society has taught you, and also dealing with complicated emotions, to pinpoint whether you're just having a difficult time or polyamory isn't for you as a whole. Even if you do have some feelings of regret, polyamory may still be the right choice for you. There are a few things I encourage people to think through if they're not sure if polyamory is for them:

Things to Consider

Work through the following questions on the theme of 'regret':

- Have you ever experienced regret in polyamory?
- How did you cope with regret and when do you feel that it becomes an issue that you need to address?

....

....

....

....

....

SCENARIO 15: EMOTIONAL RESPONSIBILITY

One of the reasons that non-monogamy attracts some people is that it can give them the freedom they want. For some, it means that they have the freedom to move in and out of other people's lives in different ways. These types of partners are often referred to as 'comet partners' – people who don't come around frequently but are considered partners. There is usually an agreement with the other partner that this is the form their relationship will take, though.

I do think that sometimes people use polyamory as an excuse to avoid emotional responsibility in relationships. While people can have romantic and sexual relationships for all sorts of reasons, if the relationship is clearly defined, then there isn't necessarily any issue around it. However, when things aren't clearly defined, people often, and understandably, go into a romantic and sexual relationship expecting some level of emotional support from their partner. While the level of emotional needs people have will vary, it's not unreasonable to expect your partner to give you some emotional support. While many people stereotype polyamory as for people who can't 'commit', polyamory involves multiple commitments, not less commitment.

Things to Consider

Work through the following questions on the theme of 'emotional responsibility':

- What is your definition of emotional responsibility, and what does 'emotional responsibility' look like in your relationship?
- Could you have a comet partner or are you a comet partner?
- What do you think the emotional expectations are within your relationships?
- Do your emotional expectations in relationships change based on the partner, or have they changed the more you have practised polyamory?

....

....

SCENARIO 16: COMPULSORY COMPERSION

If you have been involved in the polyamory community or you've read a decent amount of polyamory material, you may have heard 'there is no one right way to do polyamory,' and while I definitely agree with that, I do feel that there is an unspoken pressure to feel 'compersion' – defined as the opposite of 'jealousy', or being happy for your partner's romantic successes. This pressure can be felt within someone's community, or they may place it on their own shoulders.

It's not uncommon for people to feel that even if there is not a *right* way, the *best* way to practise polyamory is one where you experience the least amount of sadness, jealousy or 'negative' feelings about your partner dating others, or about your partner's other partners.

Many people already feel that they are 'too much' emotionally, and worry that their emotions will mean that their partners will no longer want them, or that they aren't able to 'do polyamory'. The pressure to feel happy about your partner dating other people can sometimes cause more anxiety than the simple fact of your partner being with somebody. And I have personally mischaracterized my neutral feeling about my partner being with others as jealousy, when it wasn't at all.

Some people may feel this pressure and others may not at all – it depends! But being honest with yourself about the pressures you feel within communities, and pressure you put on yourself, helps you cope with this a lot better.

Things to Consider

Work through the following questions on the theme of 'compersion':

- Do you feel compersion?
- Do you feel a pressure to feel compersion?
- How do you feel about this pressure and how do you cope with this within your relationships?

....

....

SCENARIO 17: LACK OF COMMUNITY

In the past, I have defined polyamory communities as a 'postcode lottery' – a UK-based expression which means that the quality of what you get can really differ based on location. It's not necessarily just about being in a small town or a large town. Even larger cities can struggle with the effect of being in a postcode lottery.

Being non-monogamous in a smaller or more conservative surrounding can be incredibly isolating in a lot of different ways. If you don't mesh well into the community that is immediately around you, then you can feel trapped, or only have partners who are so far away that you're unable to see them frequently.

For many people, it can be impossible to ask their current friends for advice, or even talk about their relationships, without feeling judged or for their friends to think that non-monogamy is the central problem.

Situation

You have a few partners, and you live in a mid-sized city with a large polyamorous community, but you don't really mesh well with the community. You've had some experiences with the leaders of many events that didn't sit well with you. They aren't necessarily unsafe to be around, but you're not really interested in being around them.

At times you do tend to have difficulties that crop up with your partners and at present you're not able to afford regular therapy. You had an experience with some free therapy, but the therapist suggested that non-monogamy was the main issue and that breaking up with all but one of your partners would solve the problem. Your friends who are monogamous and some of your family members are generally supportive, but they don't know how to help in these situations.

How do you handle the lack of immediate community around polyamory? Do you feel there are other communities that you can rely on when you're struggling?

....

....

SCENARIO 18: INDEPENDENCE

Many of us live within a culture of self-reliance that encourages independence. While there is value in independence and learning to be a resilient human being, I do sometimes feel there is a culture of shame around seeking out help, reassurance and being 'too emotional' or 'too needy', and this shame is amplified for different types of people in different ways. It's not bad to seek out reassurance from other people.

We've drifted a little too far, in my opinion, into the realm of independence to the point where I believe a lot of people are extremely hard on themselves for having what are basic and typical needs. While this may not affect everyone, I know that many people really struggle with the idea of 'bothering' their partner with their emotions or feelings – and this is also true within the realm of monogamy.

This can cause problems within relationships, because when we're worried about being 'too much' and we ignore our own emotions, they don't often just go away. Our needs amplify and the problems often become a lot worse and a lot bigger than they were before.

Things to Consider

Work through the following questions on the theme of 'independence':

- Do you feel a pressure to not 'bother' your partners with your emotions?
- When do you feel that you need to reach outside of yourself and ask for help from others?
- What, if anything, prevents you from asking for help from other people?
- If you have struggled with this in the past, what changed and helped you reach out when you needed it?

....

....

....

....

Theme: Compromises

SCENARIO 1: PREFERENTIAL TREATMENT

While we may talk to our partners about our other relationships, sometimes it's difficult to know where the boundaries lie, especially if we began relationships as close friends. Because non-monogamy doesn't come with a cultural script, many people default without thinking about it to complaining to one partner about their metamours.

Many of the questions that I field concern people being very involved in managing the relationship between their partner and their metamour, or feeling that they want to step in for the sake of their partner. Sometimes they do this without realizing, but other times there are situations where their partner doesn't take ownership of their choices, so the metamours are left to negotiate the boundaries in relationships that they aren't even involved in.

Situation

You're dating someone casually who has another partner and they have expressed an open preference for you over their other partner. They have done so either through a shared friend who let you know or directly to your face. In general, you feel very up and down about this relationship and sometimes really struggle with it.

How would you deal with a partner expressing a clear preference for you over another partner, either directly to your face or through a friend? Do you feel you have specific preferences for different partners, or have you in the past?

SCENARIO 2: POWER DIFFERENTIALS

It's not uncommon for us to be attracted to our partner's partners. Whenever you're dating two people who have an established relationship, regardless of whether you consider yourselves a 'triad', there is a power differential there that must be considered.

Quite often people seem to want to operate without 'hierarchy', but what they end up doing in the process is ignoring the power differentials in relationships. It makes sense when you have a partner who has another longer and more established relationship with someone else to be worried about where you might stand. It also to a certain extent makes sense to want to 'save', if you're ever put in that situation, a relationship that you have invested a lot of time and effort in.

If you're dating two people with an established relationship *together* – as a triad – then this can bring with it some added complications. People often want a triad when they start out in polyamory, but the expectation that you will have the same feelings towards both people at the same time is often unrealistic and unfair.

Situation

You're dating two people who are not only dating each other but are also married to each other. You don't necessarily define this as a 'triad'. You met them independently of each other and they practise a more parallel form of polyamory, though they personally share a living space together that they've both invested in and have a child together.

You feel a fair amount of anxiety about their established relationship, even though you don't all hang out together. Nothing has come up which has made you feel that they are prioritizing each other over you, but you've yet to discuss it and they claim not to have a hierarchy.

How would you address, or do you in your current relationships address, this power differential? Would you chalk this up to your own personal anxieties and try to ignore it? Does this feel like a hierarchy to you? How do you define a hierarchy?

. . . .

. . . .

SCENARIO 3: ATTENTION IMBALANCE

It is easy to see inequity in monogamous relationships, particularly because we have ongoing cultural commentary about the way inequity manifests itself in these relationships. But because we lack that cultural commentary in non-monogamy, I often find that many people feel extremely awkward about addressing inequity, even if it's very obvious and happening right in front of them.

Not every relationship needs to be completely and wholly equal all the time. Sometimes one partner has more needs than the other. Even in monogamy we might have times where one person may have more needs than the other or need more support than the other.

However, I've frequently said that, though I was very paranoid about feeling jealous and experiencing the pain of jealousy, I found it far more difficult to witness a partner give to other people the things I wanted from them.

Situation

You and a partner have a shared friend who is interested in both of you and thus far, things have gone well. Everything outside of the bedroom seems fine but when there are sexual situations between all three of you, over time your shared friend and your partner seem to have focused more on each other than on you.

You didn't address this in the beginning because at first you felt you might be experiencing typical jealousy and didn't want to ruin the mood. But over time, it's become more and more of an issue. Because there isn't such a stark difference outside of the bedroom, it's also making you wonder if there isn't really a problem.

Sometimes, because you spend time individually with both partners, you don't really even remember it's an issue until you are all together in bed again. Neither one of your partners have brought it up or noticed that you might not be 100 per cent during your time together.

How would you address an unspoken inequity in this situation? In what way do you feel it's best to bring up an issue like this?

SCENARIO 4: UNEQUAL NEEDS

As mentioned previously, not all relationships end up balancing out 50/50 in every single case (or 25/25/25/25 – however you choose to divide it). As someone who has a potentially degenerative condition where I could lose my sight at some point, I've always been aware of the ways that I may rely on other people in the future.

Furthermore, not having many family connections in relationship contexts has sometimes made me feel like I'm starting a little behind other people in terms of diversifying my sources of emotional support. While I have learned that having family in your life doesn't always mean you have a source of emotional support, there are lots of ways that we can either begin in relationships with 'more needs' than others, or develop this over time. It's worth thinking about how these situations might affect our current relationships.

Situation

You have previously preferred to have a more parallel style of polyamorous relationships, taking special care to balance out your time as equally as possible between all your partners. However, you become ill and one of the partners who lives closest to you steps up to help take care of you during this period.

It's not an illness that goes away in a few days and you continue to need support. Support is mostly and more easily provided by the partner who lives closest to you, though your other partners do step in and help now and then. You don't have the funds to afford a private nurse or an assistant who would be able to help you.

How would you experience this temporary imbalance of needs? How might this change if you apply it to your current situation? What if this illness became more permanent and you needed this type of support in the long term, and couldn't immediately get a carer or any type of support worker? How might you experience this as one of the partners who can't provide a lot of support? Or the partner providing the support?

....

....

SCENARIO 5: BLATANT HIERARCHIES

Hierarchies are often seen as a negative thing in many polyamory communities. Our current cultural context tells us that romantic relationships are more important than friendships. But, having to choose between a friend and a partner at the risk of losing one of those relationships is actually a very rare and distressing situation. Unless someone is forcing us or there is an emergency, we do not consciously choose one relationship over the other.

But within polyamory, because we don't have a cultural script, a lot of people end up defaulting towards what they have learned from culture in either preferring or, without intending on it, prioritizing a romantic relationship that has been established for longer or involves living together over other relationships. At the same time, though, many people take the people they live with for granted.

Does this mean that hierarchies are an issue? Generally, unspoken hierarchies or power imbalances that go unaddressed are where a lot of problems end up surfacing. Still, many people choose to operate in a non-hierarchical way because they understandably feel it aligns best with their ethics.

Situation

You have an interest in a person who has explicitly told you that they have a hierarchy, and they will prioritize your metamour over your relationship and any other relationships that they choose to have. Your metamour doesn't identify as polyamorous and is monogamous to the person you're interested in – but this isn't the first time the person you're interested in has dated someone else. Your partner has said that this hierarchy has not been an issue in previous relationships they've had with others.

How do you feel about this situation? Would it change if the prioritized partner also identified as polyamorous and dated others? Are you okay with some types of hierarchy up to a certain point? Would you need more clarity about what it means for the person you're interested in to 'prioritize' another relationship? If you do operate within hierarchies and you see yourself telling this to future partners, what obstacles do you think this might raise for them?

SCENARIO 6: AGREEMENTS AND FLEXIBILITY

Whenever people are considering polyamory, I encourage them to think about what their 'ideal' polyamorous setup is in terms of the physical realities of polyamory. How many partners do you want to have or see yourself having and in what ways will you spend your time? I also encourage couples who are opening up to figure out how they will compromise on different ideals and what the physical realities are, and to act on that as early as possible.

Scheduling intentional time together is an important aspect of any relationship, including monogamous ones, especially when a lot of people have many other struggles and demands on their time. Even when we schedule intentional time, it is common for something to come up and our plans need to change. When this happens again and again, then it starts to become a concern.

Situation

You and your partner have very demanding jobs and schedule a weekly date night to make sure you have time to reconnect each week. Many weeks can go by where this weekly date night is the only time that you have together. You and your partner both have other partners as well.

Imagine something has come up and your partner needs to cancel. They haven't ever cancelled before, unless they were ill. This clash involves another partner rather than illness or work. You won't be able to reschedule for a different time, so the only option is to cancel it.

How flexible are you around cancelling or rearranging time spent together? At what point do you feel things start to tip the other way and there are too many cancellations?

. . . .

. . . .

. . . .

. . . .

. . . .

SCENARIO 7: UNDIVIDED FOCUS

You have probably heard of a policy where, if you're out with friends, the first person who reaches for their phone has to buy a round of drinks. Laptop-less cafes are popping up in a lot of cities and we're all becoming painfully aware of how attached we are to our devices, which can have an impact on our romantic relationships.

While giving your undivided focus is generally seen as a sign of consideration, for some people this may be a really difficult thing to do. Whether because of having a very demanding career, coping with a mental illness, neurodiversity, or a different reason, a lot of people struggle to focus purely on a single activity at a time, and although it's not personal, it can often feel that way to the other person. There may also be stressful events going on in a person's life that make it difficult for people to focus on one thing for a period.

Things to Consider

Work through the following questions on the theme of 'undivided focus':

- Where do you draw the line in terms of your dates and intentional time together being interrupted by phone calls, texts or internet browsing?
- Do you need intentional time or undivided attention from your partners?
- Do you feel that your boundaries around this are different depending on the type or length of the relationship?
- Would you have different feelings around this for different partners?
- Would you have different feelings if the time being spent distracted from you or your date was focused on another partner?

....

....

....

....

SCENARIO 8: THE VETO

For those unfamiliar with the term, a 'veto' within polyamory is basically when one of your partners asks you directly (or sometimes demands) that you break up with another partner. Typically, this happens within an established 'couple' where one partner is struggling with polyamory and 'vetoes' someone's additional partner; however it can happen in a lot of other contexts. The 'veto' is typically maligned within the polyamorous community. The partner 'vetoing' another relationship is typically seen as controlling and potentially even abusive.

However, in the years of giving advice, I've found a few situations where someone wishes to enact a 'veto' in ways that aren't necessarily about being jealous of another relationship or trying to control their partner. For example, if they feel that their partner is in an abusive relationship, they can struggle with what to do in response, and think that enacting a 'veto' is their only option to 'fix' the situation. There are some situations where the metamour is incredibly hostile, or situations where someone feels like they're losing their partner to someone else, and a veto feels like the last but only resort.

Things to Consider

Work through the following questions on the theme of the 'veto':

- Are there any situations where you could understand why you or any partner would want to enact a 'veto'?
- What would be the difference for you between a 'veto' or a specific request and just bringing up a concern about another partner?
- What would be the difference to you between a 'veto' and your partner feeling that they can no longer stay with you if you stay with another partner?
- What specifically is it about the 'veto' that you would take issue with – if you do have an issue with it?

....

....

SCENARIO 9: RELATIONSHIP CHICKEN

It can be difficult to be the partner who is pursuing another relationship while your partner is struggling with difficult feelings. Some people start off in polyamory as a couple, with a rule or a hope that both people within the original couple will find partners at around the same time. It becomes difficult when one person has 'success' and the other doesn't. From what I have seen, it is more common than not for one partner to have more 'success' than the other.

When that type of situation happens, sometimes there are also rules around the 'progression' of other relationships and a lot of understandable feelings around being left behind or abandoned. This means that the partner who is within the relationship that is 'progressing' may struggle to identify when it is 'going further', especially without the typical signs of progression that a monogamous relationship may have. The result is sometimes what I call 'relationship chicken', where people end up in a situation where they feel that they have to end one relationship to avoid it 'colliding' with another.

Things to Consider

Work through the following questions on the theme of 'relationship chicken':

- Do you foresee having or have you had pressure to 'slow down' or even stop another relationship until your partner finds their own relationship?
- How do you navigate what feels like a 'competing' interest when you want to continue a relationship, but your partner is having a lot of issues with it?

....

....

....

....

....

....

SCENARIO 10: MEETING NEEDS

There is a common idea shared in many polyamorous communities that one person cannot possibly meet all of another person's needs, and expecting such a thing is unrealistic. I feel this concept is kind of misplaced and misused. While I don't think that someone should rely on a single romantic partner for every single emotional need they have, and believe the encouragement to do so by society is what causes a lot of tension in many relationships, I also don't think asking your partner to open your relationship because they don't meet all your needs is a great sell.

Monogamy may not work for some people, but, even with a 50 per cent divorce rate (and that's assuming we believe that relationships are only successful if they last until one of them dies), monogamy clearly works for many, many people.

Whether intentionally or not, assuming that one person can't meet another's needs is a slight put-down for monogamy. Non-monogamy is a different, but not inherently better, way of doing relationships in the same way that deciding to have children is a different, but not inherently better, way of building a family. We're able to validate both of those choices without putting down the other.

Things to Consider

Work through the following questions on the theme of 'meeting needs':

- What sort of needs do you feel romantic relationships fulfil in your life?
- What aspect of 'monogamy' does or doesn't meet the needs you feel you have?
- Is being non-monogamous about needs for you?
- What do you think about the idea of partners 'meeting needs' in general?

....

....

....

SCENARIO 11: DIFFERENCES AND INCOMPATIBILITY

Not all people who are interested in non-monogamy or who identify as polyamorous are innately compatible. There are multiple ways to do polyamory and not all of those are inherently compatible with one another. Someone who is more interested in solo polyamory – a form of polyamory where they do not tend to live with partners – may not work well with someone who has an interest in having a 'primary' partner.

Someone who practises a more parallel form of polyamory – where their relationships are separate from one another – is unlikely to be compatible with someone who is interested in kitchen-table polyamory – where they want their partners to interrelate frequently.

And then the typical differences that come up within monogamy are also there within polyamory. Some may want children while others don't. Some may want to live with a partner while others don't.

Things to Consider

Work through the following questions on the theme of 'incompatibility':

- Do you have a preferred style of polyamory that you can see yourself doing?
- In what ways are other types of polyamories compatible with the way you would like to do polyamory?

....

....

....

....

....

....

....

....

SCENARIO 12: EXCLUSIVITY

One of the things we learn through a monogamous-centric culture is that exclusivity is what makes something special. Choosing one partner who is the 'best' or preferring one person over everyone else is the centrepiece of a lot of monogamous love songs. One of the reasons why a lot of people struggle to identify what their 'progression' is within a polyamorous relationship is that the biggest aspect of what defines someone being 'official' within monogamous-centric culture is the exclusivity.

This does carry over into polyamory, with or without a hierarchy. Some people prefer to have one partner that they have a romantic connection with, while others prefer to have one partner who they live with, or one partner who they have children with, or make other major life decisions with. None of this is inherently a problem, especially if it's clearly communicated to every person involved. Not everyone necessarily wants to be the partner someone has children or a house with.

However, the concept of exclusivity can be applied in lots of other ways within polyamory that help make specific relationships special. The way one applies these rules can cause a lot of different and understandable feelings – and even the feeling of unexpected exclusivity can create problems.

Situation

One day your partner takes you on a date to a new romantic restaurant. It's a wonderful and memorable evening that you feel has made your connection grow. You could see this restaurant becoming a place you might consider for more special events, even an anniversary dinner.

The next week, you find out that they have taken another partner on the same date to the same romantic restaurant you went to before. You can't help but feel a little ping of jealousy. Neither one of you defined this restaurant as particularly special or exclusive, but you can't help feeling sadness from wanting this place to be something special between the two of you. As illogical as you feel it is, there is something about them going to the restaurant with the other partner that makes it a little less special, and you can't put your finger exactly on why.

You don't want to request this become 'your restaurant', and at this point it's a little too late anyway, so what do you do in this situation? How would you manage these feelings? Does this feel big enough to discuss with your partner, or would you work through it on your own? If you were in the reverse position, how would you want your partner to discuss this with you?

SCENARIO 13: AGE GAPS

It's not uncommon for people to be introduced to polyamory when they're already in a relationship. For some people, especially those who come from smaller towns or more conservative backgrounds, they may not actually become introduced to polyamory as a real, viable option for them until much later in life, after they have already established long marriages, had children, and shared property ownership with someone else.

For this reason, polyamorous communities can have a variety of ages of people present or even have a sort of dichotomy of people who discovered polyamory in their 40s and 50s and people who came across non-monogamy in college. I would say, in my experience, as you can find in the queer community, you can run into situations where people who are just starting off in non-monogamy at an older age are still getting used to the concept of non-monogamy, despite their maturity and life experience, in the same way that younger people are.

However, age gaps are something many people have strong opinions about, for understandable reasons. Due to my experience as a youth worker, I can see legitimacy in the critique of large age gaps in relationships but also understand why a large physical age gap may exist where a large emotional age gap does not, and why that might make that relationship more equitable than people might think.

Situation

You have one partner at the time and both of you are in your mid-20s. Your partner begins dating someone who is 25 years older than they are who is new to polyamory and just out of a very long-term relationship. You and your partner don't necessarily have any long-term plans together and you haven't really talked about anything solid in the future. You're mostly just still getting to know each other.

In general, you don't have any big plans or want to have the typical established things that many people have in a relationship, so there isn't a bigger issue of being worried about another partner being more 'established' than you are.

Does the issue of age difference here have an impact on you? Would it be different if you were both in your mid-30s? For what reasons would you have an issue with age gaps? Explore the concept and consider different situations in which you are the partner with the age gap, and your partner has an issue with it.

SCENARIO 14: DON'T ASK, DON'T TELL

One of the things that's discouraged in a lot of polyamorous communities is 'don't ask, don't tell' relationships (DADT relationships). This refers to a relationship where two people who are in a monogamous relationship agree to a tentatively open relationship where one of the people in the couple is allowed to have other outside sexual relationships, but the other partner doesn't want to have any involvement or even know about the other relationships. They may have an agreement where one night a week they are free to do whatever they like, and one person doesn't ask and the other doesn't tell.

Usually, this setup involves not progressing past sexual relationships with the other partners, though they may be allowed to have romantic relationships as long as they still prioritize their primary relationship over any other connections they have. A lot of people feel this agreement is inherently problematic and refuse to take part in it. There is an obvious power differential in this arrangement in terms of what relationship is prioritized over others, and that understandably creates an issue for a lot of people.

Things to Consider

Work through the following questions on the theme of 'DADT relationships':

- Would you enter a DADT relationship?
- Do you feel like DADT relationships contradict any of your values or viewpoints?
- How would you feel if your partner agreed to a DADT relationship with someone else?

....

....

....

....

....

....

SCENARIO 15: SOCIAL POWER

While one can have a good deal of self-confidence, social conceptions and misconceptions can have an impact on our dating lives and a lot of that can be influenced by social power. Dealing with the discrimination we've faced growing up, or continuing to face that discrimination as an adult, can have an obvious tangible impact on our mental health.

Anyone who has done even a cursory amount of research will be able to see that different forms of discrimination can impact not only how people feel about themselves but also make dating a struggle in various ways. Discrimination can be extremely obvious and blunt, or only come out through other aspects of relationships and dating. Depending on where you live, even going on dating sites may be a struggle. Even if this isn't something your partner can control, it can still make things difficult within your relationships.

Situation

You have a partner who faces a lot of discriminatory attitudes within their workplace and their dating life in your local area. Moving to a different city or changing jobs isn't really an option for them. Although they do see a therapist, it sometimes weighs heavily on them. They often don't want to attend events or do much online dating because of these issues.

You have dealt with discrimination previously, but not on this level or in the same way as your partner. You're always there to support them but you feel that you're not able provide the support they need to get through this situation, and you can tell that it weighs on them.

How do you handle these types of differences within your relationships? What do you do to support your partner through difficult situations? How do you feel social power affects your relationships and dating life?

....

....

....

....

SCENARIO 16: CARE EQUITY

Most people are aware that having children has a huge impact on people's day-to-day lives, as well as the amount of time they can give to any given relationship. Furthermore, living together creates a certain number of responsibilities that can't be avoided. Even when people are in monogamous relationships, it's important for people to actively discuss the time they spend on childcare and home care as individuals and make sure that each adult is actively taking part in the development of the child or the upkeep of the home as best as possible.

Unfortunately, I have seen many situations in polyamory (and monogamy) where there has not been a thorough discussion of childcare or home care responsibility, and this responsibility weighing on people can take its toll. Overwhelmingly, I do see this situation impacting women more within polyamorous relationships, though it could impact anyone.

It's important to discuss expectations of home care and childcare together way before it becomes something that builds up resentment.

Things to Consider

Work through the following questions on the theme of 'care equity':

- Have you experienced an inequity in terms of providing childcare or home care in your relationships?
- How might you address an imbalance in your relationship with childcare or home care?
- How comfortable do you feel negotiating more time for yourself or for other relationships if you need to?

....

....

....

....

....

SCENARIO 17: LOSING TOUCH

There are a lot of aspects around our life that affect our relationships that are out of our control. If something happens with work or family, suddenly a lot of our time could be redirected without us having much control over it. Often there is a dislike in polyamory of situations that 'control' our relationships, but there are many things outside of our control.

We've all had the experience of friends slowly slipping away from us. With partners, this is a little less common in monogamy, although occasionally partners absolutely do grow apart over time. It can be more difficult to pinpoint when this situation is happening with a partner who lives apart from you or happens to be struggling with something in their life right now.

Situation

One of your partners with whom you like to spend a lot of your time has been lately growing more and more distant. They are not as available as they used to be for either in-person, digital or phone time spent with you.

When you ask why this is the case, your partner says that one of their other partners is requesting more and more of their time recently, but that this may not change. It's starting to affect how close you feel to them, but you don't know if it's the best time to say that. Whenever you get together, it seems so rare that you don't want to 'spoil' your time together discussing something so sad.

How would you manage this situation? What might help with organizing more time with your partner? How would you feel if the reverse was happening, and you felt you had less and less time to spend with a partner?

. . . .

. . . .

. . . .

. . . .

. . . .

. . . .

SCENARIO 18: TIME MANAGEMENT

As mentioned previously, there are lots of different ways to be polyamorous. The only thing that's true for most types of polyamories and non-monogamy is that you are accepting a situation where your partner may not spend as much time with you as they might in a typical monogamous situation.

This can be true for people in monogamous situations who have partners with time-intensive careers, hobbies, or anything else that pulls them away from their partner. So I encourage people to ask themselves if they could or would want to be part of that type of monogamous relationship before getting to all the additional complexities of non-monogamy. You could be the least jealous person in the world, but if you want to spend a lot of time with your partner, non-monogamy may not work for you.

For some people who go from monogamy to non-monogamy, even after they agree they are non-monogamous, not much tends to change in their day-to-day lives. I encourage people to think about the physical realities of non-monogamy even before they find other partners if they will be moving from a situation where they spend a lot of time together to one where they will have less time to spend together.

Things to Consider

Work through the following questions on the theme of 'time management':

- In what ways have you managed shifting, if you have, from a lot of time with a partner to less time with a partner?
- How do you plan your physical time with your partners? What if anything has a direct impact on that?
- Is there a minimum time you feel you need to have with partners in order to maintain your relationship?

....

....

....

....

SCENARIO 19: LEGITIMATE CONCERNS

As previously discussed, the 'veto' is very often demonized within polyamorous communities. When giving advice, I've seen a lot of different situations where people feel very trapped and feel that a veto is the only way out. Ultimatums can function in monogamy in the same ways.

There are a lot of situations that don't pop up within monogamy unless there are extremely dire situations or issues with family. In a monogamous relationship, someone may have a difficult family situation that's creating problems within the relationship, or they may have a friendship that isn't working out well and is causing friction. But in both these situations, there are lots of ways to create boundaries around the situation that might address the issue. And on the whole, people don't tend to spend a lot of time with their families.

But within polyamory, if you have an issue with your metamour that feels valid and you are genuinely concerned about your partner's wellbeing, there don't seem to be too many options. Obviously, you can put up boundaries around you spending time with your metamour, but there is only so much you can do about your partner spending time with them. It's unsurprising, then, that a lot of people feel like a veto is their only option.

Situation

One of your partners has begun seeing your ex. Normally, this wouldn't be a big issue, but this isn't just any ex. You feel that you're still recovering mentally from the relationship with that ex, and you're very concerned about the mental health of your partner. While you are willing to believe that people can change and get better, your relationship didn't end that long ago and as far as you know, your ex hasn't sought therapy or addressed any of the issues that you feel they would have needed to for you to believe that they had changed.

You're not interested in exercising veto power, but you're genuinely concerned and it's beginning to make you feel extremely anxious. Would you address this with your partner? If so, how would you address it? How would you feel if the roles were reversed, and your partner was concerned for you?

Theme: Sexuality and Infidelity

SCENARIO 1: STARTING WITH CHEATING

Often, if someone is already within a couple and has thought about opening their relationship or being non-monogamous, even introducing the concept is fraught with potential problems – especially for couples who have already been together a long time, and have children and/or shared assets. There are many who would feel so hurt by the idea that their partner is interested in non-monogamy that it could end the relationship.

Rare opportunities, such as an old high school sweetheart being recently single and looking for a partner, can spur a person within a closed couple to ask about opening the relationship. This can sometimes create a unique pressure on an already difficult situation as people may not only struggle to adapt to non-monogamy or attempt to see if it works for them, but also need to deal from the start with a metamour who, in a way, 'caused' this change. Or they may feel pressure to be 'okay' with the transition so the other partner can take advantage of the opportunity.

Situation

You can approach this scenario from one or both histories: either you and your partner have been in a monogamous relationship for a very long time, or you have recently connected with someone and began a monogamous relationship with them.

Recently, your partner has met someone that spurred them to ask you to open your relationship. They didn't hide this at all from you, and discussions began almost immediately. You felt a little nervous about the change but were somewhat open to the idea. After a lot of back and forth, though, you suggest that you separate instead. Your partner confesses that they have already cheated with the person they were interested in.

How would you feel in this situation? Would you feel comfortable opening the relationship and your partner dating someone they had cheated on you with? Given the situation, could you see yourself forgiving your partner, or would this be too difficult for you to recover from? Would the situation change if you had a long-established relationship versus having got together fairly recently?

SCENARIO 2: FOUNDATIONAL TRUST

The foundation of any relationship is trust, which is usually built over time as you get to know one another and go through conflicts or situations that test your bond. Whenever we have a set social script, as is the case within monogamy, not tripping over boundaries and violating trust can be a lot easier – though I do think that people should discuss things like how they define 'cheating', because this can often be a source of trust violations.

But within polyamory, without a sociocultural script, boundaries are sometimes less defined, or we're exploring how we want to have relationships and what our boundaries are. Sometimes we don't even know we have a boundary until it's already been crossed.

Many people think that we're often too quick today to dump a partner rather than put work into relationships, and others sometimes believe that relationships should be perfect and work without conflict. When you're navigating something new, it can be easy to accidentally violate a boundary or agree to something you don't actually want to do. It can be difficult to know how to balance wanting to forgive partners with your own boundaries and needs.

Things to Consider

Work through the following questions on the theme of 'trust and forgiveness':

- What is your personal limit on forgiving incidences where your trust was violated?
- How important is it for you that your trust was violated unintentionally, rather than intentionally?
- Are there any specific behaviours that you feel are 'unforgivable' and why?

. . . .

. . . .

. . . .

. . . .

SCENARIO 3: DELAYED DISCLOSURE

Many people unfamiliar with polyamory are surprised to find out that cheating is possible within polyamory. It is usually defined as having another relationship or an encounter that you hide from your partner – though definitions of what 'cheating' are can vary. There may be some polyamorous relationships where there is no such thing as cheating if those in that relationship have agreed.

This is often complicated by being unaware of the exact moment when a relationship becomes 'more' when there are rules about needing to disclose to partners when a relationship 'progresses'. I have always told people to expect disclosure to be awkward, but I've heard of many situations where people have accidentally cheated in polyamory simply because they weren't sure how to get over the awkwardness. Not to mention, when you have actually done something with someone else and have to tell your partner, it's no longer a theory but a practice. You will be seeing your partner's real reaction to the reality of the situation instead of just the idea that you *might* be with someone else at some point.

Situation

You and your partner don't have any set rules about disclosure of new relationships. Over the time you have been together, you have usually let each other know about new dates within a few days of scheduling them. You've also been able to let each other know before having sex when a new sexual experience has happened that changes the sexual health risk in the relationship.

However, you recently went through a death in your family or immediate social circle and struggled with grief, calling on a few of your partners for support and pausing a few developing relationships. During this time period, which lasted a few weeks until you felt a little more stable, your partner had a new date with a fast-forming connection, but avoided telling you because they felt that the priority was supporting you in your grief. Your partner has now had two dates with this new person.

How would you define this situation? Would this be considered 'cheating'? Would it change if there had been a sexual experience involved? Where are your personal boundaries around this? How might you handle disclosing a new relationship if your partner was going through something similar?

SCENARIO 4: SEXUALITY

People on the asexual spectrum could be interested in polyamory without necessarily wanting to have multiple sexual relationships with others. Many people say there is no 'one right way to do polyamory' but I've personally found in many communities that if I wasn't interested in having a sexual relationship quickly, some people immediately lost interest in developing a relationship with me.

This isn't to say that asexual people can't have an interest in casual sex or developing sexual relationships quickly, but it's important to highlight for people who are on the ace (asexual) spectrum that it can sometimes feel like there is an unspoken hierarchy within many polyamorous communities where if you're not interested in or immediately ready to have sex, you are deprioritized.

Many ace polyamory people also feel that it can be difficult to avoid comparing themselves with partners who can offer a sexual relationship if that is not something that they are interested in offering.

Things to Consider

Work through the following questions on the theme of 'the role of sexuality in relationships':

- What role does sex play in your relationships?
- How important is having a sexual element in all your relationships?
- Would you be open to a non-sexual partnership?
- In what ways might you consider being intimate with a partner without sex?

SCENARIO 5: WITNESSING INTIMACY

Polyamory communities, even in larger cities, tend to be small worlds and many people, especially in more conservative areas, can be hesitant to try polyamory, or may be hesitant to date people who are new to non-monogamy. This means that events and parties within the communities might be the only places where individuals can interact with others who are polyamorous.

Many parties may also contain a sexual element, which means that you may not only go to the same party as one of your partners but even accidentally witness your partner being sexually intimate with someone else. While for some people, this isn't an issue and might be a positive element of going to the same party (though I think it is important to make sure that the metamour involved is okay with the voyeuristic aspect of it), for others this could cause them understandable trepidation.

Especially where there are few places people can go to socially interact with polyamorous people, and where you don't want to control what parties your partners go to or miss a chance to attend yourself, there can be a lot of understandable anxiety around this. I have personally found that the pressure to not have a 'reaction' to seeing my partner even kiss someone else is often more uncomfortable for me than the reality of seeing them do anything. Likewise, the idea of having to comfort an upset partner who's had an emotional reaction to seeing something might make the prospect of going to the same party daunting.

Things to Consider

Work through the following questions on the theme of 'witnessing intimacy':

- How does the idea of witnessing a partner be intimate with someone else land with you? Does this depend on what level of intimacy you witness?
- Do you think there are any strategies you can employ to help you cope with any emotions you might suddenly feel witnessing your partner with someone else?
- How would you feel if the roles are reversed?
- Do you think that you would like to make agreements with your partner about what events you do or don't go to?

SCENARIO 6: OPPOSITES ATTRACT

Differences in relationships are to be expected, and people can be fundamentally interested in non-monogamy for different reasons and still be compatible with each other. Sometimes these differences can cause a lot of anxiety. Even when monogamous, people are encouraged to compare themselves to other people and to see themselves as the 'best' choice their partner made.

Within that framework, monogamous people can be worried about how they compare to previous partners. Within polyamory, it's a lot easier to be worried about your partner comparing you directly to other partners. It's also a lot easier for you to be worried about being replaced in a situation where your partner is actively with other people. People who are more familiar with polyamory may not feel this as strongly as people who are brand new to it, so none of this may be a concern for you now.

Either way, it makes a lot of sense that people can have a lot of anxiety about the differences they have with their partners.

Situation

Let's say that one partner in a relationship is extremely interested in non-monogamy for sexual freedom and enjoys having a lot of flings and casual affairs while the other is more reserved, very rarely attracted to other people and even sometimes worried that they might be monogamous. The more reserved person is a little worried about whether they are too boring for their partner, or that their partner will find someone who is more interested in flings.

In another relationship, one person's interest in non-monogamy is focused on building romantic relationships whereas the other person's interest is more in having a variety of sexual experiences, but they want few deep connections and maybe even only want the one deep connection with the other person. The first person gets a little anxious when there is a new love on the horizon for the other.

How would you manage anxieties in either scenario? The relationships still function well between these two people, but the differences in approach can cause a little fear. Do you see yourself reflected in any of these people? If these issues have cropped up in relationships before, how have you managed these anxieties?

SCENARIO 7: SEXUAL COMPARISONS

Sexuality occupies a different space in all our lives. For some of us, it's an integral part of intimacy with our partners and for others it's something that they enjoy with people regardless of their level of intimacy with the individual involved. For some of us, it's a huge part of our identity and our emotional expression, and for others, it's a small part of our lives that isn't any more important than anything else.

As I've said previously, it's easier in polyamorous and non-monogamous situations to directly compare yourself to others and even to feel a lot more threatened by the presence of metamours than one would in a monogamous situation by exes and previous relationships. Sexuality is one of those things where comparisons can be particularly emotional and complicated.

A lot of people feel that sex overall is something that one can 'master' even though different people like different things. Many people struggle with basic communication because they believe they ought to be able to read their partner's mind to demonstrate their 'skill' at sex when it's much simpler for them to just ask what it is that their partners want. Sexuality itself is used to sell many different products on the premise that being sexualized in the right way or being good at sex will earn you the love you cherish.

And bluntly, sometimes there are situations where someone has better sexual chemistry with one partner than another, which is no one's fault but can be difficult to ignore.

Things to Consider

Work through the following questions on the theme of 'sexual comparisons':

- Do you find yourself comparing yourself to your metamours sexually, and is this something that really concerns you?
- Do these feelings change depending on who your partner dates or even what they look like? Be honest!
- Would you want to know if your partner compared you to other partners? In what way?
- How do you address these feelings with a partner?

SCENARIO 8: INFIDELITY HELPER

One of the things that you discover whenever you read through stories about people coming out to friends or family about being non-monogamous is that there is a strange subset of the population that seems to be much more open minded and willing to accept infidelity than non-monogamy. Some people also understand infidelity a lot better than they understand non-monogamy.

While this may seem strange, there is a long history of infidelity being normalized within multiple cultures. In fact, when marriage was less about romantic love and more about property exchange and power, it was extremely common for people to have affairs outside of their marriages – though usually this type of behaviour was only permissible for certain types of people. Understandably, a lot of non-monogamous people are already extremely frustrated by the idea that non-monogamy is cheating, so the fact that some people accept infidelity more than monogamy can be more than a little frustrating.

Situation

You have reconnected with an old flame from your previous school years via social media and managed to catch up with each other randomly when you only had one current partner. While you aren't hiding that you're non-monogamous, your status all over your social media is that you have a current relationship, and many people assume that you are monogamous to your partner unless you correct them. It's very likely that your old flame knows that you are not single.

Before you're able to have a discussion with them about your situation, they begin sending you very flirty messages and eventually invite you out to what is an obvious one-to-one romantic date. It's stated overtly, but reading between the lines, it's obvious that they know that you're with someone and it's unlikely that they know about you being non-monogamous – so they are perfectly fine with helping you cheat on your partner. That fact makes you more than a little uneasy.

How would you deal with this situation? Would you feel comfortable being with someone who is fine with helping you commit infidelity? Would you tell your partner about this? How would you feel if the situation was reversed, and your partner went through this? Would you want your partner to tell you if this happened? Would you feel comfortable if your partner slept with this person without telling them they were non-monogamous?

SCENARIO 9: DESIRE DIFFERENCES

Differences in sexual desire and frequency are so common in partnerships that I often encourage people to expect it rather than to expect to have the exact same preferences as their partner. However, polyamorous situations allow for people to have a variety of partners – including people who have absolutely no interest in sexuality at all. In situations where sexual incompatibility might be a cause to completely end a monogamous relationship, a polyamorous setup could allow those differences to matter a lot less.

While some people need sexual experiences within their relationships, the fact that polyamory focuses mostly on building romantic relationships leaves open the possibility for asexual people to find partnership with others who are not interested in sex within relationships. But whether partners are asexual or not, differences in desire can also cause a lot of anxiety within relationships.

Things to Consider

Work through the following questions on the theme of 'desire differences':

- How often have you found you have differences with partners in terms of sexual desire?
- Have you felt this was something to explore or something that you deal with on your own?
- Does the difference in sexual desire cause you or your partners anxiety? How do you manage that?

....

....

....

....

....

....

....

SCENARIO 10: STIS

Sexually transmitted infections – or STIs – are one of the risks of having sex, and they aren't something that can be completely prevented. One can use condoms, dental dams, gloves, and other protection and while condoms do prevent against a good number of STIs, a few STIs, including HPV (human papillomavirus), are transmitted through skin-to-skin contact, and therefore could be transmitted even if one were to have sex through clothing.

Most STIs are curable through antibiotics or antivirals, and a select few stay in the body for the rest of your life. However, quite often it is the stigma of sexually transmitted infections that causes more issues than the STIs themselves. If someone has been diagnosed with HIV, for example, medication and treatment can prevent the virus being transmitted to anyone else. Pre-exposure prophylaxis, a medicine that reduces your chances of getting HIV, is also available for people in high-risk groups.

According to the Centers for Disease Control, not only is HPV the most common STI, but there is also no test to find a person's HPV 'status' and most people don't even know they have it. For most people, HPV doesn't cause any health problems and often goes away on its own. Many people are unfamiliar with STIs and their risk factors, and most of their fear comes from a lack of education about them rather than the facts.

Things to Consider

Work through the following questions on the theme of 'STI exposure':

- Have you ever researched which sexual activities involve more risk of certain STIs and why?
- What do you feel is 'risky' in terms of sex acts?
- What STIs are you particularly concerned about and why?
- How did you grow up understanding STIs? If your attitude has changed, in what way?

....

....

....

SCENARIO 11: BARRIER NEGOTIATIONS

Although there are a lot of different opinions about having rules in polyamory, quite often there are very clear rules and boundaries around sexual health risk. While no one can eliminate the risk of exposure to sexual health risks completely, there are approaches one can take to prevent the spread of infections.

It's important to be informed about the risks of different types of sexual acts and to speak with partners about what they define as 'risky' and what your boundaries are. Furthermore, when you and your partners discuss risk, you may find that you don't agree on how to define it. Beyond just the concept of using barriers to prevent against pregnancy and some STIs, you may find that when you delve into the complexities of different sexual acts, your definition of what you're willing to risk, with who, and why, might actually wildly vary between you and your partner. Relying on just a concept of 'no risky sex' may not actually serve either of you and may need to be discussed further.

Situation

You begin dating someone who has an immunocompromised partner. They have strict rules around any barrier-free sex. They ask not only that you use extensive protection for all sex acts with them but also with your other partner. While you feel that that is a bit of an unusual request, you have no problem complying with those rules and your other partner doesn't mind either.

However, a few months later you begin dating a third person who wants to have some low-risk barrier-free sex with you and is not happy about the idea of having to use extensive barriers because of a relationship that is so removed from them. It feels to them like their metamour is controlling your relationship even though you have no issue with using extensive protection.

How would you navigate this situation? If the partner was not immunocompromised, how would this change your answer? Are you immunocompromised and do you feel this impacts your rules are around sexual health barriers?

. . . .

SCENARIO 12: SEXUAL SLIP-UP

As mentioned previously, not everyone identifies the same sexual acts as 'risky'. To add to complications, because some sexually transmitted infections (STIs) can't be detected until six months after exposure, and some can be permanent, once a boundary has been crossed and the risk has been taken, there is little one can do to undo it.

It's important to also remember in our discussions about sexual boundaries and sexual health risk that some people in different cultures, notably within the United States, have not had much education about sexual risk and/or have been terrified into believing that all sex is incredibly risky. Very few people have a good understanding of sexual health risk, all the different types of sexually transmitted infections, and how they are transmitted between partners.

As a result, even though a lot of sexually transmitted infections are either curable, incredibly common or manageable, many people who have an STI feel an enormous amount of shame, particularly with HIV (human immunodeficiency virus) and HPV (human papillomavirus). It's important to remember that, while we're allowed to want to avoid catching a sexually transmitted infection, most of them are either curable or extremely manageable.

We need to put the risk into context. Driving comes with a certain amount of risk and can result in permanent, irreversible injury or death, and yet we consider the value of driving to be worth the risks. We could take a similar attitude towards sexuality. This comparison can help us re-examine our perspective around our assumptions about risk and how we react to that risk.

Situation

You and a partner have an agreement to always have 'protected sex', mostly to prevent pregnancy, and that has never been an issue.

After your partner returns from a visit with a metamour, you find out they had unprotected oral sex, which to you falls outside of the realms of what you agreed. They believed that you meant only penetrative sex would be protected.

When you express that you'd have to abstain from unprotected oral sex from them for a few months, they shrug, not seeming bothered. You're not necessarily upset about the confusion, especially since you hadn't identified what 'protected' really meant, but the shrug hurt.

What would you do in this situation? Do you define what 'protected' means with your partners and what risk is? Would you abstain in response to the situation?

SCENARIO 13: CASUAL VERSUS SERIOUS

We define our relationships in a variety of ways, and how that plays out in polyamory can be interesting. I've been in situations where I would define a connection as being more serious than my partner defines it, and while that didn't cause me too much anxiety and fear, I can understand, especially for people who want to know how their partner views the relationship, why differing definitions might be confusing or anxiety provoking.

When you're working from the lens of monogamy, where there is exclusivity and a cultural script around what a relationship is built around and how it 'progresses', it's a lot easier to identify what a casual as opposed to a serious relationship represents. But within the standpoint of non-monogamy, how one defines 'serious' and 'casual' and what that means can really differ from person to person.

Even if a relationship is 'casual', that doesn't necessarily mean that the person we have a relationship with isn't meaningful to us or that the relationship doesn't mean a lot to us.

Things to Consider

Work through the following questions on the theme of 'casual and serious relationships':

- What defines a casual relationship to you?
- What defines a serious relationship to you?
- Are you interested in more casual or more serious relationships or both? And why?
- Do you experience anxiety when your partner has a new casual relationship or a new serious relationship or both?

....

....

....

....

....

SCENARIO 14: PUBLIC DISPLAYS OF AFFECTION

As previously discussed, there are lots of complications that come into play when witnessing your partner being intimate with someone else. However, witnessing something sexual can be different than just witnessing your partner kissing or doing any normal public displays of affection (PDA) that one might typically do when with a partner. Even in these cases, I often find that the pressure to be 'okay' with everything makes me more uncomfortable than any PDA I have witnessed.

That pressure definitely crops up in shared environments with your partner and your metamour. In many cases, I have told people to expect awkwardness because it's unlikely one would be prepared for a situation like this. In addition to this pressure, we already lack a cultural script for non-monogamy, so it's understandable that, unless we have a particular interest in seeing these PDAs, this might be difficult to navigate.

Equally, your partner may also have difficulty figuring out what the appropriate boundaries are and whether PDA should be avoided or not when with both you and your metamour. It's easier to get it out on the table to discuss rather than trying to walk on eggshells.

Situation

Your partner has come to you with an issue about a dinner you plan on having with both your partner and your metamour. This is their first experience with polyamory and they're not quite sure how to navigate the situation. They really want you and the metamour to get along well but they also don't want to cause any upset, either for you or the metamour involved.

They ask you what your feelings are about public displays of affection both towards you and towards their metamour. They haven't yet asked their metamour about this, but they plan to. Should they avoid showing too much affection towards the metamour? If you're fine with it, what if the metamour isn't? Would you be okay with them showing less affection towards you if their metamour felt weird or awkward?

How do you feel in general about public displays of affection in shared spaces with metamours? Does your attitude change depending on the type of event or the type of affection you're likely to witness? Has your attitude changed over time?

SCENARIO 15: COWPOKING AND EXPERIENCE

While I'm not sure this is a very common phenomenon, a few people have experienced something called cowgirling/cowboying/cowpoking, where a person who is monogamous enters into a relationship with a polyamorous person with the intentional purpose of 'turning' them monogamous and 'stealing' them from their partner. It's sometimes hard to tell whether this has been done intentionally or whether, after experiencing different relationships, they just decide to leave one partner and go monogamous with another.

Cowpoking is just one of many reasons why people hesitate to date people who are new to non-monogamy or who don't have 'experience', or even avoid these relationships entirely. While I understand this reluctance to date people who are new to non-monogamy, whether it's out of fear of cowpoking or just general concern about some of the new emotions that often come with trying out non-monogamy for the first time, I'm always encouraging people to reconsider the idea that more time being non-monogamous inherently means that you're 'better' at relationships.

Things to Consider

Work through the following questions on the theme of 'experience':

- How do you feel about cowpoking? Do you think only dating people with 'experience' will prevent this type of thing from happening?
- Do you feel like you're 'safer' with people who have 'experience' in non-monogamy?
- Would you avoid dating someone who was completely new to non-monogamy?
- What do you feel 'experience' in non-monogamy brings you? How would you apply this to monogamy?

. . . .

. . . .

. . . .

. . . .

SCENARIO 16: ONE PENIS POLICY

Another unliked concept within most polyamory communities is the 'one penis policy', or OPP. Typically this involves a heterosexual cis couple who usually, but not always, started off as monogamous and opened their relationship but have a rule that the woman in the couple is only allowed to date other women. This isn't usually something that the woman has introduced into the relationship, and the idea is that the man in the couple doesn't feel threatened by other women and therefore is only okay with his partner dating women.

While I don't necessarily agree with the idea of this being an official rule, especially because these 'policies' rarely if ever consider non-binary and/or trans people, I absolutely have been in positions where I found myself being less anxious about my partners dating people to whom it was harder to compare my body and gender directly. Especially because of my feelings that my gender identity isn't valid, when my partner dated women, my brain would tell me that they would prefer someone with a 'normal' gender and 'normal' body and therefore leave me for a 'real woman'. No such dialogue crossed my brain when my partner dated cis men.

Furthermore, I have seen a lot of situations where women are interested in non-monogamy mostly because they want to explore new relationships with women rather than men. And while these situations also don't necessarily make room for non-binary identities or trans people, I think it's different when a woman *chooses* to only date other women rather than being dictated to by someone else.

Things to Consider

Work through the following questions on the theme of 'OPP':

- Would you ever consider an OPP? Do you have a policy like this but without it being an official rule?
- Would you date someone who had an OPP with someone else?

. . . .

. . . .

Conclusion

If you're new to non-monogamy, there's no easy way to prepare yourself for trying it, in the same way that there's no way to prepare yourself for any major life transition like parenting or moving to a new country. By putting together some of the common situations and scenarios you might face, my hope is that you can think through some of these situations before they arise.

Sometimes discussing these scenarios with a potential partner can help you align on your boundaries and make you consider things you may not have thought about until further down the line. There aren't always 'right' answers to some of these scenarios. They come down to the compatibility between yourself and your partners. As I often say in my column and podcast, sometimes you don't know that you have or need boundaries until they've already been crossed.

My hope with this workbook is that you feel a little more prepared, whether you have a partner or not. Or if you're already non-monogamous, I hope this book helped you explore some potential scenarios and work out the different ways you could deal with these situations. Or, at the very least, I hope this workbook has provided some good exploration of different topics you hadn't considered before.

As I say in the column and podcast, I hope this helped and good luck.

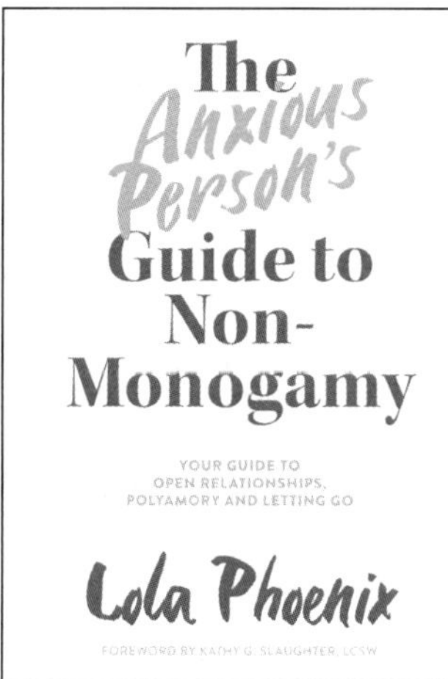

The Anxious Person's Guide to Non-Monogamy

Your Guide to Open Relationships, Polyamory and Letting Go

Lola Phoenix

Foreword by Kathy G. Slaughter, LCSW

£14.99 | $19.95 | PB | 208PP |
ISBN 978 1 83997 213 3|
eISBN 978 1 83997 214 0

Embarking on a non-monogamous relationship can be a daunting experience, opening old wounds that cause anxiety, fear and confusion – something Lola Phoenix knows about all too well.

In this all-you-need-to-know guide to exploring non-monogamy, polyamory and open relationships, Lola draws upon their years of experience in giving advice and being non-monogamous to provide guidance for every stage of your journey, helping you to prioritize your mental health and wellbeing along the way.

Beginning with advice on starting out – such as finding your anchor, figuring out your 'why', challenging your fears and practising self-compassion – the book proceeds to cover the emotional aspects of non-monogamous relationships, including dealing with jealousy and judgement, managing anxiety and maintaining independence, as well as practical elements such as scheduling your time, negotiating boundaries and managing your expectations, all accompanied with activities for further exploration.

Whether you are new to non-monogamy, or have been non-monogamous for years, this insightful and empowering book will provide you with the emotional tools you will need to live a happy non-monogamous life.

Lola Phoenix runs the popular weekly relationship advice column and podcast, Non-Monogamy Help, and has been non-monogamous for over a decade. Their writing has appeared in Medium, Huffington Post, PinkNews, Gay Star News, The Independent and Everyday Feminism.